Love
in the
Gospels

Love
in the
Gospels

by
A Modern Pilgrim

THE THOMAS MORE PRESS
Chicago, Illinois

Materials in this book appeared in different form in the newsletter *Markings* published by the Thomas More Association.

ISBN 0-88347-138-8

Contents

Continued on next page.

Contents

1
God Speaks Through Others

Modern Scripture experts give us interesting background to the gospel story of the threatened stoning of the woman caught in adultery. It does not appear in any early versions of the Old Testament, and is apparently even an addition to the gospel in the form in which we presently have it. Some suggest that it was cut out of Luke's gospel and restored at a later date in John's gospel, which was written many decades later. But despite its dubious history, virtually all writers today are agreed that it is undoubtedly an incident that actually happened during the public life of Jesus. Why the story's peculiar history? Many early Christians found it scandalous. Jesus seems too permissive; he seems to be taking a "soft line" on adultery. The early Christian leadership was morally quite rigorous; they were afraid that the ordinary faithful would be shocked by the permissiveness of Jesus, so they suppressed this incident lest it scandalize the faithful.

We have grown so familiar with this story that its threatening import may be lost on us; but if we stop to think about it for a moment, it becomes clear that the story is potentially very dangerous. Most of us were raised in an environment where the sins of the flesh were far and away the most terrible kinds of sin. Even the "legitimate" sexual pleasure between husband and wife was considered to be "necessary" but much better left unmentioned. Yet in the gospel Jesus rather casually absolves someone from a violation of the sixth commandment without the person even expressing any sorrow. It would appear that Jesus did not consider this such a terrible sin at all. Indeed, he was harsher on the cruel and hate-filled men who were going to execute the woman than he was on her sinfulness. A dangerous man, this Jesus, preaching moral laxity and shattering some cherished convictions about what the "worst" kinds of sin are. Jesus seemed to think that hatred was worse than "immorality."

Unlike their Greek and Roman counterparts, the Jews at the time of Jesus did not despise the human body and did not view sexuality as a necessary evil at best. The comparsion between sexual union on the one hand and the love of God for his people, on the other, was to be found in the Hebrew scriptures several hundred years before the coming of Jesus. But even by the somewhat liberal sexual standards of the Jews, Jesus was permissive. He associated with prostitutes and sinners, he had close friends who were women, he did not denounce adultery as the worst of sins, and he rejected the double standard by which women were more harshly judged than men. Not to respond to God's love was for Jesus the worst sort of infidelity; but a sin of the flesh he seemed all too ready to forgive.

Many in the Church today seem to be obsessed by sexual morality; others feel that the only advice one can give human beings in matters of sex is not to sin. What else is Christianity all about, after all, but opposition to "immorality?" For such people the casual attitude of Jesus must be a profound scandal, for Jesus seems to be suggesting that loving generosity is more important that "purity." If Jesus had preached that kind of doctrine today, he might very well find himself blamed for the "sexual revolution."

For most people the temptations to adultery are only intermittent. The logistical and time arrangements of adultery are so complicated in our society that most of the time, for most men and women, it is not really all that serious an alternative. The real problem is not so much overcoming the temptation to sin with others as overcoming the temptation to permit one's own love life to deteriorate into monotony, routine, insensitivity, indifference. As one contemporary writer puts it, for most married people the real challenge in marriage is not staying out of someone else's bed but rather living up to the challenge of one's own bed.

We learn through the gospels that God speaks to us most insistently through the other human beings who people our lives. The most challenging invitations from God come from those who are "beloved others," and particularly from the one to whom we are committed in marriage (at least for most people). The point for those who are seeking to respond to the call of God as it is revealed to us in our sexual partner is not that adultery is easily forgiven, but rather that we live in a universe created by a generously loving God who not only expects loving generosity from us in our response to those others who represent him but who will reinforce, underpin, and validate that generosity. The important point about sexuality is not that it has great potential for sin, though it does, but rather that in a world where the most serious sin is to refuse to be lovingly generous, sexuality provides one of the greatest opportunities available to humankind for loving generosity.

Despite the alleged sexual revolution, despite all the talk about permissiveness, despite the plethora of sexual manuals, despite the availability of soft-core and even medium hardcore pornography on the local newsstands, despite all the talk about sex, the truth of the matter still is that most married couples find it very difficult to speak to one another about their intimate relations; indeed, they are more than a little put off even when the subject is raised in the Sunday homily. What does that (sex) have to do with religion? It should be clear in the context of the gospel that it has everything to do with religion, and religion has everything to do with it. The challenge of God and the beloved other, the God who speaks to us through the other, are Christian beliefs that to be taken at all seriously—and, of course, they must be taken seriously—must mean that a husband and wife cannot refuse to discuss their intimacy. Such a refusal is in its own way even more sinful than adultery, for that, as we see in the gospel, is a sin Jesus could forgive easily.

2
God's Love and Ours

To be loved is to be astonished, surprised, amazed, overwhelmed. Someone really does love us! At first it seems too good to be true. Then we realize that it is true, and the goodness of it makes the whole world beautiful, and our hearts catch fire with joy. The sky is bluer, the grass greener, human voices richer, the stars at night filled with secret messages. We are loved, and all is perfect.

The most dramatic experience of being loved usually takes place in the years of young adulthood when a young person discovers that the person he or she loves actually returns that love. In an earlier day, we were very blasé and cynical about young love; it was something that happened during the 1950s, part of the Mickey Mouse Club era, something that occurred in those happy days when folk heroes like the Fonz walked the earth, and one could afford naive notions of love. Of course, whatever the cultural fashion, young people do still fall in love and do still feel that it is an experience they have discovered for the first time. If they are constrained to disguise the sweetness, the freshness, and the novelty of their love by cynicism or pseudo-sophistication, the reason may be that they are trying to protect themselves from the hurt and disillusionment they see have poisoned the lives of so many of their elders. They keep their excitement about discovering that they are lovable and are loved to themselves, lest they be ridiculed as naive fools.

But being loved is still a surprise. To discover that one is loved is to learn that despite all one's fears to the contrary, one is still worth loving. The other must see in us some things that we do not see ourselves—some goodness, some attractiveness, some appeal that we have missed or that we only dared to hope that we had. For the other to love us means that we are not only as good as we had hoped we might be but perhaps—in their eyes, anyway—a little bit better. And while the experience of being loved may be most explosive and most dramatic in romantic, affectionate young adults, it is indeed more powerful and more lasting in the later years of life when we have gone beyond both illusion and disillusion and discovered that the other still loves us, still supports us, still believes in us, still finds mystery, wonder, surprise and enchantment in us. Such an experience of being loved touches us in the very depths of our souls.

Many of us were told when we were younger that the love God feels for us, the love Jesus manifested in his life on earth, the love we Christians are expected to have for one another, according to the gospel, is very different from the romantic love we saw in the movies or on television or, if one goes back far enough, heard on the radio, or sung about in popular songs. There are two different kinds of love, the love ordinary humans experience in ordinary circumstances and the special kind of love, denatured, refined, cleaned up, that is appropriate for religious matters and for church communities. For ordinary human love, you see, is too raw, too elemental, too fierce, too uncontrollable, too powerful to be appropriate for such things as how God feels about his people and how members of the church ought to feel about one another. There is in the relationship between God and humankind and among members of the church no room for passion.

But such a distinction is absurd. Love is love—sometimes quiet and gentle, sometimes raw and elemental, sometimes a spring breeze, sometimes a winter storm—but always powerful, pervasive and beyond the control of neat, orderly reason. If there be any difference at all between God's love for us and the love of a man and woman for one another, it is that God's love is wilder, more passionate, more uncontrollable, more demanding, more fierce. And while loving support of members of the church for one another obviously does not find the same expression as does the love of a husband and wife for each other, it is still true that the loving concern between two spouses who are permanently enamored of each other is the model and paradigm for all commitments within the Christian community. We who are followers of the Lord Jesus must care for one another with a powerful, intense, deep and permanent concern.

Father Martin D'Arcy, in his book *The Mind and Heart of Love,* says that love is not so much possessing someone else as that the other person is caught in the fierce grip of a concern for our happiness. It is an awesome experience—rewarding but terrifying, ennobling but frightening, reassuring but challenging. It is what relationships in the Christian community should be like—in due proportion, of course, and in the right times and right places with the right people, but still clearly the goal of the Christian life. As the Lord loves us, so should we love and be loved by others who are part of his flock.

3
The Gratuity of Love

In one of D. H. Lawrence's short stories a young doctor walking through the countryside observes a girl, apparently in a trance, walk into a pool and quickly sink over her head. She is a morose, rather unfriendly person whose brothers are friends of the young man. The whole family is about to leave that part of the country because of financial setbacks. Without a second thought he dashes down to the pond, wades in over his head and pulls out the now unconscious girl. He carries her to his home and revives her. The girl is so overwhelmed by the discovery that he has risked his life to save hers that she becomes convinced that he must love her. Her passion is contagious and the young doctor discovers that indeed he has begun to love her. Frightened of what she says, the girl tries to draw off from the commitment; but the young doctor, now thoroughly in love, will not listen to her. He loves her and that is that.

The short story "The Horsetrader's Daughter" has exactly the same theme as the parable of the shepherd who risks the rest of his flock to pursue one lost sheep. It's a bizarre, absurd, foolish investment of time and energy that can in no way be justified by the cost. Similarly, in another parable, to neglect nine silver pieces for the pursuit of one piece is an absurd risk. You are probably not going to find the lost piece and in the meantime you could easily lose the other nine. Finally, having found the one lost piece of silver your neighbors are going to think that you are utterly crazy when you call them in to celebrate the fact you've finally found a lost fifty-cent piece. The point of the parable, however, is that God's behavior, judged by human standards, is crazy. God's love, like all real love, does not count the cost, does not act rationally, does not behave sensibly.

The young doctor in D. H. Lawrence's story had never found the woman attractive. His impulse to prevent her suicide was sudden and unreflective. Falling in love with her as he held her soggy, battered little body in his arms was lunacy. When her brothers found out they would certainly laugh at him, and the people in his district would be baffled as to why a promising young practitioner should fall in love with such an odd girl. His affection for her was as crazy as that of the shepherd pursuing the worthless sheep, the woman hunting for the trivial coin, the father of the prodigal son going down the road to greet that returning wastrel. But that's the way love is; it hedges no bets, counts no costs, computes no formulae, calculates no interest rates; it simply loves and that is that.

Is not Jesus inconsistent? One time he advises us to calculate very carefully what we're getting into before we follow him. Another time he tells us that love does not calculate but rather is absurd and irrational, lunatic and half-mad. Why the apparent contradiction? In fact, first Jesus was talking about us and later talking about the heavenly Father. Given our own weaknesses and frailties, he warns that we had better calculate carefully before we respond to the absurd, whimsical, half-mad love of God for us—at least half-mad by our own human standards of calculation. God has no more "business" falling in love with us than the shepherd has going off hunting for the lost sheep, or than D. H. Lawrence's doctor had falling in love with the strange, moody horsetrader's daughter. God does it just the same.

There is something wildly reckless about the God that is portrayed in these parables of mercy. He has parties over foolish things to celebrate unimportant events. He showers good things on sinners before they can even adequately express their compunction. He engages in foolish and frantic searches which, if we were to undertake them, would make us an object of ridicule. There is something just a little bit berserk about this God of ours. As a matter of fact, this bizarre behavior of his is almost embarrassing to us. Surely Jesus must be engaging in some kind of oriental, rhetorical exaggeration. He cannot expect us to believe that God literally rejoices over each individual one of us no matter how worthless we may be.

However, we must remember that the reality of God's love for us is *underestimated* by the story of the crazy shepherd or the foolish woman celebrating the discovery of a lost half-dollar. By human standards, God's love is even wilder, more unfathomable, more absurd than the fixation of the shepherd on the single sheep or the woman on the lost coin or the young doctor on the pathetic girl. To say that God is fixated on us is not to exaggerate but rather to speak something less than the full, rich truth.

4
Conflict and Reconciliation

The most deadly disease that can affect any love relationship is self-righteousness. When lovers begin to store up grudges, to count hurts, to file away unkind words, to keep track of injuries and affronts, then their relationship is in deep trouble. When one or both can remember the harsh words, the thoughtless deeds that happened five, ten, fifteen years ago, then a deadly poison is killing their love. Remember, for example, in the novel *Trinity*, two decades after the birth of their first son, the Ulster Protestant husband still remembers that his wife turned to her father rather than to him in her first childbirth. We are struck by the poignancy of such a fictional incident because we are aware of how truly good we human beings are at opening up our minds and hearts to the poisonous self-righteousness of remembering the offenses of others and forgetting our own.

It would be a mistake to think that in the parable of the publican and the Pharisee Jesus is putting a white hat on the publican and a black hat on the Pharisee. He is not saying that the publican is a good guy because he broke all the rules and the Pharisee a bad guy because he kept all the rules. Jesus is not saying it doesn't matter whether you keep the rules, but, he is saying there is more involved than rules. The authentic Christian combines the piety of the Pharisee with the humility of the publican. The point of the parable is that all the piety of the Pharisee is worthless without the humility of the publican. Love does not thrive on righteousness, love does not thrive even solely on doing all the required things; love succeeds only when we are willing to admit, as a prelude to reconciliation, not other people's mistakes, but our own.

In the fierce, defensive combativeness that seeps into almost any human intimacy, we defend ourselves by attacking the other, we protect ourselves from facing the ugliness of our own faults and failures by toting up a record of the other's failures and confronting the other with it. Curiously enough, the other does exactly the same thing, and the relationship deteriorates into vindictiveness, anger, punitiveness, and narrow bookkeeping of who was to blame for what unpleasant incident. Jesus says to us, in effect: "You may be able to get away with that in human love relationships, but it will destroy them in the process. But don't think you'll be able to play accountant with my Father in heaven. Virtue and piety he takes for granted, though he is willing to forgive you when, like every other human being, you have failed substantially in those areas. What he wants is generous and open humility, and if you don't have that, then your detailed records may impress the Internal Revenue Service, but they won't impress him one bit."

If we have any wisdom at all in human intimacy, we know that reconciliations take place not when we can extort by brute force the other person's admission of responsibility for troubles, difficulties, and conflicts but only when we are able to take the initiative toward restoring full love by acknowledging our own responsibilities. Humility, not self-righteousness, is the secret to the growth of human love, as well as the secret to growth in our love relationship with God. The only obligation we impose is the obligation on ourselves to admit our faults, our failings, our weaknesses, our foul-ups, our insensitivities, our contributions to monotony, boredom, weariness, and frustration.

Clearly we make ourselves vulnerable when we display humility in a relationship with another. The Pharisee is secure in his relationship with God; he has kept his part of the bargain. Now he self-righteously demands God's response. The publican is totally vulnerable; he concedes his own foul-up and throws himself on God's mercy. He is taking a terrible chance, is he not, that God will turn on him, laugh at him, will say in effect, "How can you possibly expect me to forgive someone as worthless as you?" In human relationships we know that vulnerability is a terrible risk. The point of the parable is that in our relationship with God it is not. Indeed, far from being a terrible risk, it is the secret of the whole love affair.

But vulnerable relationships, we know from our human experience, are risky—more rewarding, more exciting, more pleasurable, more growth producing, but also more dangerous. We much prefer to protect ourselves against stern, rigid barriers of self-righteousness, of remembered deeds, of a carefully detailed past. With such protection we can deal with lovers—either human or divine. It is not as exciting, not as pleasurable, but it's a lot safer. So the Pharisee thought; so think the Pharisees today.

5
Risk-Taking

Because we are contingent creatures who did not have to exist and who at some time—almost any time—may cease to exist (at least in our present form), we humans are careful, calculating, cautious beings. We plan for retirement, we invest in life insurance, we innoculate ourselves against diseases, we enter relationships with other human beings very cautiously, revealing ourselves slowly, hesitantly, if at all. There isn't any other way a self-conscious, contingent creature can behave. But we know full well that the best moments of our life are those moments when we throw caution to the winds and behave impulsively—though not necessarily irrationally. It is probably impossible for us to be impulsive and spontaneous very often in life, and it might be dangerous. Still, life's best moments are those of breathless risk-taking.

Jesus seems to have had a special affinity for risk-taking people, for the spontaneous, the reckless, and the impulsive. Persons like Mary Magdalene, Simon Peter and Zacchaeus made fools of themselves, and the more cautious and careful observers in the audience must have laughed at them—at least up their sleeves. They were passionate and reckless people whose passions got them into trouble, but whose passions also seemed to get them out of trouble. Zacchaeus must have been a passionate, ambitious, aggressive person. He piled up his money recklessly, he gave it away recklessly, and most recklessly of all, he climbed up that tree and made a fool of himself just so he could get a look at Jesus.

How did Jesus respond? Did he laugh? Did he make fun? Did he ridicule? Did he point out Zacchaeus as the kind of man who was a slave to his passions? No. On the contrary, while he doubtless smiled at Zacchaeus—who could help but smile at Zacchaeus?—he also came to his house and had supper with him. Zacchaeus—blundering, blithering, babbling, loud-mouthed fool—was Jesus' kind of people.

Falling in love and giving oneself to another in intimate relationship, then opening oneself up completely to the other when one discovers that that is the only way intimacy can be sustained are all reckless, foolhardy, lunatic things to do. We human beings are driven to them occasionally by our physical or psychological passions, but our fears and cautions are so great that we count the risks, pull back, hedge, tread carefully. Even though spontaneous generosity and openness seem almost always to pay dividends, we are not usually about to take the chance of doing it again. One can count on it, the next day Zacchaeus found it hard to be as foolhardy and as reckless in his relationship with his wife and family as he had been the day before with Jesus. The habit of calculated restlessness only predisposes us to take chances in our love relationships; it never makes it easy.

Even the words "calculated restlessness" seem like a contradiction in terms. Zacchaeus, however, was not a fool; he was far too successful an entrepreneur to be that. He took risks, he was passionate, he was restless; but he was not mindlessly or stupidly so. Climbing up a tree to see Jesus of Nazareth was a foolhardy thing, but it turned out not to be foolish at all. The secret of a successful human life is not merely to follow one's instincts blindly but to know what instincts should be restrained and what ones should be surrendered to. The cautious, conservative person surrenders to none of his instincts and leads a narrow, rigid, dull life. The recklessly foolish person surrenders to all his instincts and leads a life of chaos and disaster. Somewhere in between is the appropriate human life, choosing carefully which instincts are sound and then giving oneself over completely to them.

In human marital love is the reflection and the tracer of our love affair with God. In human marital intimacy there are usually three critical turning points when either or both partners are impulsive and reckless or the love cools off and becomes routine. The first moment is that of spontaneous physical and psychological attraction in which two people decide they like one another; the second moment, far more serious and far more difficult, is when they decide they like each other well enough to cast caution to the winds and recklessly commit themselves to spending the rest of their lives together. The third moment, even more frightening, is that moment when the couple discovers that the only hope for the growth of their love is that they become even more reckless and abandon their punitive, vindictive defensiveness with regard to each other and take the biggest leap of all—the leap of a life together in which there is no pretense, no hiding, no paralyzing fear, no covering up, no hidden agenda, no reserve behind which one can take refuge.

This paradigm, or model, of human love is very like the similar pattern of our relationship with God. Zacchaeus was attracted enough by Jesus to climb the tree; he then found himself with an uninvited dinner guest, and then, finally, he threw aside all pretense and committed himself totally to a life in the service of the Lord —a commitment which then would have to be renewed on each subsequent day. We discover the attractiveness of God, we are tempted (perhaps one could even say "seduced") by God, we decide to commit our lives to a belief in his loving goodness. Then, as trouble and difficulty and suffering and tragedy happen in our lives, we are tempted to pull back the trust and find security in ourselves and not in him. Then, finally, we make the biggest leap of all, deciding that we will trust God's loving goodness no matter what happens. We become Zacchaeus at the dinner table, and we have surely become Jesus' kind of people.

We are not the Zacchaeus kind of person in our relationship with God, however, unless we can be as calculatedly spontaneous, as carefully reckless, as rationally foolhardy in our relationships with other human beings as Zacchaeus was in his relationship with Jesus. Do we really risk ourselves with others? Then we have also risked ourselves for God.

6
Saints in Love

Saints are strange people. Simeon Stylites sat on a pillar for twenty years. Vincent Ferrer was forbidden by his religious superiors to work miracles, so he kept a man who had fallen from a roof suspended in the air while he got permission from those superiors to work one more miracle. Catherine of Siena told off popes. Francis of Assisi was the first streaker. Thomas More and Philip Neri tended to be practical jokers. By and large when one goes through the list of saints and considers them objectively, one might well have second thoughts about whether it would be a good thing to be counted among their number. At least life would never be dull.

There is something a bit wild, mad, crazy about a saint. A saint may be an almost pathological worker like Peter Canisius or as relaxed and casual as John XXIII. He may be as charming as Vincent de Paul or as forbidding as Pius V, as eloquent as John Chrysostom or as difficult and obscure as Paul frequently was. He might be as brilliant as Bonaventure or as pedestrian as John Vianney. She might be as imperious as Teresa of Avila and Louise de Marillac or as withdrawn as Juliana of Norwich. There is a wide variety of styles, personalities, talents, interests and commitments among the saints. They have even fought one another as did Peter and Paul, but there is one thing they all had in common: they were all a bit mad.

What is the nature of this madness? At first it is difficult to discern. Saints seem to have more resources, be a little deeper, a little richer in their responses. They bounce back more quickly from defeat. They also see things differently. Usually saints are not starry-eyed optimists, yet they seem to be able to break through appearances more quickly than the rest of us to get to the fundamentals of a situation. Saints are able to look at the long-range, the very long-range— like eternity, maybe.

But then it begins to emerge. What is different about saints is that they are happy. It is almost as though the Beatitudes are turned on end. The saint is able to be the kind of person described in the gospel because he is happy; he is able to be a peacemaker, single of heart, meek, poor in spirit. It is not so much that the beautitudinal practices earn him or her blessedness or happiness; it is because saints are already happy that they have the freedom, the strength, the internal resources, the confidence to do things that Jesus calls us to do in the Sermon on the Mount. Saints can "crack through" the frustrations, the disappointments, the weariness of daily life and "come alive" precisely because they know they are in the grip of a passionate love which will never let them down, and that in the end nothing that they do that is good, generous, gracious is ever wasted. The madness of a saint is the madness of a person in love.

In saints, what we really celebrate is that such love is offered to us all. We can all be just a little mad, we can all have just a little bit of the saint in us, we can all be free to frolic, to laugh, to rejoice, to *live*. Sanctity is a matter of degree. The great saints, those who get canonized, are very special kinds of people. Clearly not everyone is called to that kind of specialness, but we are all still called to be special, we are all offered a chance at the happy madness of the saints. We are all given an opportunity to drink at least some of the gloriously heady wine that turned them on and can turn us into more dazzling human beings than we ever thought possible.

There was a time in the lives of each of us when that kind of divine madness was almost a reality for us. Each of us probably knows someone who in late childhood or early adolescence seemed to be possessed, however temporarily, of some of the glorious insanity that marks a saint. Then something went wrong; the person lost his or her nerve and settled for a life of timid, anxious mediocrity. We feel very sad when we think of such people because we know how much we all need them. In fact, however, opportunities like that are offered to all of us—though not in so great a degree. The wine bottle is open and sitting on the table. We can drink deeply and be transformed by the dizzy love that God offers us. It may make a drastic change in our lives, but it is a change which will make us happier and improve the lives of all around us.

It is a mistake to think that the saints are fundamentally different from us in some kind of physical or chemical way. Some of them have certain social advantages. Elizabeth Seton, for example, had a superb education, powerful friends, immense personal self-confidence. But not all the saints had such advantages by any means. The more spectacular saints, the ones that get all the public notice, also seem to have had special gifts of divine graces, but the many ordinary saints had no extraordinary talents and no extraordinary graces. They were and are fundamentally no different from us in biology, physiology, chemistry, psychology. They kept joy and wonder alive through the frustrations and disappointments of life, and it was no easier for them than it is for us. They woke up in the morning with "the blahs" every bit as often as we do. To keep their wonder and their joy alive despite the blahs of life they had to put in an immense amount of effort. They suffered many, many failures. The secret to being one of all the saints is not to exorcise the blahs from life; it is rather never to cease fighting against them.

When you encounter a saint, or at least someone who is obviously a very good Christian, the experience is much like that of a glorious autumn morning or the bright, shiny face of a happy child. It is revelatory; it reveals to us what life is all about. So it should be with our own lives. When those who are not followers of Jesus of Nazareth encounter us, they should see the joy, the hope and the surprise of the resurrection in our personality. We should ask ourselves how many of those who know us well would consider our personality to be a revelation? How many would consider an encounter with us to be like an autumn morning or a smiling child?

7
Love of Mary

Not too long ago two prominent national secular publications, *Village Voice* and the *New York Times Magazine,* contained articles on the Virgin Mary. The author of the article in the *New York Times* said that one noted modern writer thought that a religious symbol appropriate for our time was the Greek god Atlas, the god who held the burden of the world on his shoulders. But, the author of the *Times* article wrote, in any competition between Atlas and Mary the mother of Jesus, there was not much doubt, based on all the evidence of the past, which symbol would win. Whoever sang a song to Atlas? Whoever wrote a poem in his praise? Atlas, observed the author, is the name of a tire; Mary the mother of Jesus is the woman in whose honor were fashioned the most beautiful buildings humankind has ever known. Maybe Catholics have forgotten something about Mary that a lot of other people are beginning to discover.

It is not just the *New York Times Magazine* that seems to have rediscovered the Virgin Mary. Harvard's Protestant theologian Harvey Cox and UCLA's secular historian Lynn White have also sung her praises. As the author of the article in the *New York Times* suggested, oddly enough, just at a time when popular devotion to Mary seems at a low ebb in the Catholic church, our separated brothers seem to have rediscovered Mary. An agnostic writer like Theodore Roszak has even suggested that the only really good thing about the Roman Catholicism of his youth was his devotion to Mary. Many of us seem ready to give up Mary as part of the necessary price for ecumenical dialogue with Protestants or open and honest discussion with secular humanists and agnostics. Now they come and tell us that what we have just about given up is one of the strongest assets we had. Life gets very confusing at times.

In retrospect, the bitter argument in the Reformation and the Counter Reformation over the Virgin Mary seems absurd. How could Christians get themselves so blindly entangled in theological terminology and argumentation that they could be at each other's throats over the incredibly charming young woman who holds her son in her arms in the Bethlehem scene? How could they have fought with one another about the person in whose honor the glorious rose windows of the cathedrals were made? How could they have fought over the person in whose honor St. Bernard wrote the *Ave Maris Stella,* about whom many poets from the anonymous writers in the catacombs to W. H. Auden wrote and every artist from the first century to Salva-

dor Dali painted? Mary the mother of Jesus may
be the most important cultural symbol in all the
Western world and we poor, foolish Christians,
instead of being illuminated by the light and the
warmth of this glorious symbol, have fallen to
fighting over it. And we Catholic Christians,
God forgive us, in the years after the Vatican
Council, seem all too prepared to yield this symbol to the pietists on the one hand and the Protestants on the other. Now we are caught up by
the challenge of agnostics, humanists and secular theologians.

But why? Where is the power of Mary? Why
has she had such immense appeal? Why has she
been able to survive the assaults of enemies and
the demeaning sentiment of friends? The answer is very simple. Mary stands for a fresh new
start. Mary represents the capacity of the human
race to be renewed. Mary signifies the birth of a
new humanity. Mary celebrates freshness, novelty, new beginnings, the flowering of the fields,
the glorious chance to start all over again. The
Virgin Mary tells us quite simply that God loves
us.

In the Old Testament there was a style of
speech in which one person represented the
whole people. Abraham, Moses and David were
not only individual persons; they were also cor-
porate persons who represented and stood for
the entire Hebrew nation. Similarly, in the

writing of the prophet Zephaniah, the "Daughter of Zion" represents the whole Hebrew people. She may have been an actual young woman of the royal family with whom Zephaniah was acquainted, a beautiful young woman who was courted by the great kings and nobles of her time. Or she may have been merely a figment of the prophet's imagination. But the prophet saw that the people of God had the same effect on God as does an attractive young person on a king looking for a wife. Just as foreign kings sought after the Daughter of Zion because they were attracted by her beauty, so also God seeks after his people because he is attracted by their beauty.

In the gospel Luke says that Mary is the new Daughter of Zion, the new woman who has found favor in God's sight, the woman who represents the new people of God, the church, after whom God desires as a king desires the princess who will be his wife. The attractiveness of Mary represents our attractiveness as a holy people. God sought Mary to be the mother of his son Jesus; and he seeks us to continue the work of Jesus down through the centuries. Mary is the church, the new bride of God. And in her bright, fresh, young attractiveness the human race found a new beginning, for she brought Jesus into the world, and with his coming a new humanity was born, a new era was begun, a fresh new chance was given to humankind to find happiness. Mary has been attractive to all times and in all places because in her freshness and her newness we see reason to begin to hope once again.

It is a bit startling to think that Mary represents us in such a direct way, that the God who loves her also loves us, and indeed loves us in a way not unlike the way he loves her. Mary is so fresh, so beautiful, so attractive, so appealing, how can God possibly look the same way at us poor, tired, battered, weary old sinners? But we are part of his church, and Mary represents the church, and for all our weaknesses and frailties, he loves us. For in us he sees what he saw in Mary, a chance for a new beginning.

8
Rejected Love

Neil Simon's movie, *The Goodbye Girl*, was funny because it deals with an experience we all have, the experience of love being "out of phase" in our closest relationships. Each of us knows what it is like to feel like hating at a time when the other person feels like loving. The theme is an old one in comedy, dating back at least to Shakespeare and Moliere. We laugh at unrequited love because we know eventually it will be requited—at least on the stage or screen. In real life, however, the experience is often just the opposite. We offer our love in vain; either the other rejects it or we are never able to get our acts in sync with one another. The pain of rejected love eventually goes away (save for a neurotic), but when we are trapped in its pain, it seems to us that no psychological suffering could possibly be greater.

Rejected love is something we all endure. Sometimes it is minor and passing—a child or a spouse rebuffs our affection. But sometimes it is devastating. Even the superficial romances of adolescents, laughed at and dismissed when we grow older, are enormously painful in the experience; and to be turned down in a serious quest for love is as shattering an experience as anyone can have. Those men and women whose husbands or wives suddenly and seemingly without warning end their marriages, a phenomenon not uncommon in these days of blind, often selfish quest for self-fulfillment, are lucky to ever recover their balance and self-confidence. A parent who has dedicated much of his or her existence to a child is overwhelmed with sadness when that child-turned-adult ignores the parent's existence. Similarly, an adult suffers when no matter how hard he or she tries, they can do nothing to please the insatiable demands and the impossible standards of a parent. (How many mothers, for example, are ever satisfied with the way their daughters keep house?)

The one who rejects our offer of love rejects us. They seem to be saying not merely that we are not good enough but for all practical purposes we don't exist. At least it would be only a matter of mild distress to them if we vanished from the face of the earth. We have opened ourselves, made ourselves vulnerable and fragile by our offer of love, and the other has laughed at us, in effect, pushed us aside, stomped on us, broken our heart. The exclamation, "I wish I were dead," springs to the lips of the rejected lover, for the idea of going out of existence does not seem a bad one at all.

We all know what it's like for a parent when a child turns away, rejects him, ridicules him,

will have nothing to do with him. The parent—
mother or father—is devastated, overwhelmed,
wiped out, nearly destroyed. "That is the way it
is with my father in heaven," Jesus tells us,
"when you do not respond to his love. For he
loves you even more intensely than a mother or
a father loves their sons and daughters." If we
take this metaphor of rejected parental love seriously, its religious impact is enormous. No religion in the world, particularly any religion with
any claim to philosophical sophistication, can
take such a comparison seriously. What sort of a
God is it who falls in love with his creatures the
way human parents fall in love with a child? So
we do our best to take Jesus' metaphor seriously.
But how are we to behave, with a God who dotes
on us the way a proud father does on his first-
born son? Such a God would be too much altogether—a passionate, disturbing, demanding,
fiercely loving God. No, that's the last kind of a
God we want to get mixed up with.

Still, we are stuck with the metaphor of Jesus.
It is his comparison, the way he saw things.
There are immense philosophical problems that
have to be answered, and Christian philosophers have been something less than successful
in answering them. It is not easy to comprehend
how God can love us like a father loves his
first-born child; but however seemingly incom-
prehensible the comparison is, it is still the one

he made and made repeatedly in many parables. "Take the wildest, most passionate, most demanding, most fiery of human loves," he says. "Examine and experience what they are like, and you have some idea of who my heavenly Father is."

Surely, we say, Jesus is exaggerating. He really didn't mean to be taken seriously. But even a cursory reading of the scriptures shows us that Jesus didn't exaggerate and he always meant to be taken seriously. Indeed, if we were to try to persuade Jesus that his comparison of human and divine love was an exaggeration, his response would be to say, "No, if anything, it's an understatement, because the passion my heavenly Father feels for you is even greater than that which a father feels for his first-born son." In other words, don't try to explain the images of Jesus away; he meant them to be taken seriously, however mind-boggling they may be philosophically, and however, breathtaking they may be religiously in their demand of a response from us.

9
Seizing the Opportunity

Once upon a time, there was a rich and beautiful princess—call her Princess Leia, if you wish—who was as kind and good as she was beautiful. She fell in love with a peasant boy—you can call him Luke Skywalker. Her father (we'll change the story and call him Obi Wan Kenobi) also liked the young peasant very much. He said to the peasant, "I'll tell you what I'll do" (or some ancient variety of that). "My daughter loves you, I love you. Marry the kid and take her off my hands and I'll make you the heir to the kingdom and the most powerful prince in the land. How about that for a deal?" And Luke Skywalker says, "Well, gee, I don't know. It's an interesting notion, all right. The princess is presentable enough, as young women go, I guess. But my friend Han Solo has some things to do—like going out into the galaxy for a little hunting and fishing. I'll tell you what, Obi Wan, old boy, I'll let you know in a couple of months."

Now we would be inclined to say that Luke Skywalker was pretty much of a fool. He was offered the opportunity of a lifetime, and while he didn't say no exactly, he didn't say yes either. He chickened out. No matter how good she was,

Princess Leia might be excused from banging him over the head with a laser sword.

Our story is unfair, you may say, because it involves the by now familiar plight of the princess from *Star Wars,* and gives it an unfair twist. Whoever heard of a beautiful princess being spurned? Whoever heard of a peasant boy like Luke Skywalker saying he'd rather go fishing and hunting than marry the magic princess? If someone is going to tell a story at all, why not tell it right?

This is precisely the complaint which people in the times of Jesus made against Jesus' version of an equally familiar story. In the folk tale the people of Jesus' time knew the vineyard workers are called to repentence by the king and respond to his call just as the Jewish people periodically responded to the call of the great prophets. With what must have seemed perverse glee, Jesus tears the story apart, has the vineyard workers kill the messengers, and then praises them for the ruthlessness with which they seized the opportunity available to them.

The moral: seize the opportunity while you have it. A vineyard that doesn't take the opportunity to produce fruit will be destroyed, and wicked men who wish to make money must be ruthless in the pursuit of it. So it ought to be with us in the pursuit of God's love. Everything else ought to take second place. It is not the deed of the wicked workers that Jesus praises but rather their single-minded dedication to their goal. A bright, ambitious man like Luke Skywalker, in other words, doesn't belong out hunting with Han Solo; he belongs at court with Princess Leia, struggling for power. All of this was another example of the mind-boggling, preconception-shattering, disconcerting style of Jesus. "What is the matter with you?" he asks the people in effect. "My heavenly Father has offered you his love. How come you do not pursue it with all the powers at your command? Why are you not pursuing it with the same dedication with which thieves pursue wealth and ambitious politicians pursue power? Jesus is saying to us in effect the same things that Princee Leia might be saying to her galaxy-bound Luke Skywalker. "Are you out of your mind? Why are you blowing this opportunity?"

People didn't like what Jesus did with their beloved story, and we are somewhat upset too. It just doesn't seem appropriate for Jesus to hold up the ambition of thieves and politicians as something for us to imitate. Why was he so interested in shaking us up? It does no good to argue with the style of Jesus. He aimed to shake us up because he thought we needed shaking up. He compares us to dedicated thieves, criminals, and murderers and finds us wanting, because, as the beer ad puts it, "You only go around once in life." To reject God in that one attempt is like being a lackadaisical thief, a shiftless politician, an unserious lover. You only get one chance at the magic princess, Skywalker. For the love of heaven—quite literally—don't blow it.

10

Love Is Tender

When many of us old folk were back in grammar school the sisters used to tell us a story: Jesus came one morning to Peter at the Gate of Heaven and said to him, "Hey, Peter, I've got a list of people I've seen walking down the heavenly streets these last couple of weeks who simply don't belong here. You know our rules. We've got high standards in this neighborhood, and I see a lot of undesirables have been getting in lately." Peter shrugged his shoulders, "I can't help it, Boss. I turn these people away at the gate; if I find them inside, I throw them out; but no sooner do I expel them from the front door than they go around to the back and your mother lets them in through the kitchen window." As children, we laughed because it was funny and we thought it was kind of neat; we knew that's the way mothers were. Now that we are grown up, of course, we know better. However, very recently, a number of Catholic writers have begun to say that maybe the old story was not all that wrong; maybe the main function of Mary in Catholic life is to represent the loving tenderness of God. Mary stands for the fact that the God who creates order, establishes rules and enforces them is also a God who cares with a gentle, loving tenderness that a mother shows when she cares for her child.

We humans soak up tenderness like a sponge. When we're babies we assume as a matter of right that the mother who holds us in her arms will always be gentle and tender. When we are little children we run to mommy with our "owies" and demand the common panacea for all owies—a kiss and a Band-Aid. When we are hurt physically or psychologically during our school years, we go back to mother for encouragement, reassurance, and warmth. In married life, husbands often turn to their wives for a reassuring, gentle, consoling tenderness they once received from their mothers; and in a happy trusting marriage, women can turn to their husbands for warm, supportive, gentle, even maternal tenderness when they desperately need it. When we are sick in the hospital we enjoy the professional but nonetheless personal care of the nurse. In every mature human being there is the capacity to receive maternal tenderness and to give it.

What is tenderness all about? Basically, it is a signal of caring; the other person cares about us and cares about us gently, reassuringly, patiently but also profoundly and even passionately. The other wants us to be happy, wants the hurts and the owies to go away, wants us to be able to stand up again and be our full, rich, warm, healthy self. Tenderness may come in periods of discouragement, it may even be a relationship of temporary dependency, but it is dependence oriented toward independence. The one who tenderly cares for us does not want to keep us dependent but wants us to get better. The mother kisses the owie to make it go away.

If every mature, self-possessed human adult has the ability to give and to receive maternal tenderness, then it would be absurd to deny maternal tenderness in God. God is as gentle, as soft, as caring, as reassuring as a mother is to a little baby, as a nurse is with a very sick patient, and as a grandmother is at the bedside of her dying son. In addition to being the father, God is also mother, spouse, and grandmother—madonna, sponsa, and pieta.

Normally we think of God as a father—frequently as a stern, righteous, just, implacable father—the one who created the whole world, keeps it going, will bring it toward its fulfillment and rather ruthlessly imposes the justice of his royal order on the universe. God is a patriarch, a difficult, touchy old man up there in the sky, enforcing law and order. Of course, this is silly. Actually, we translate the Hebrew word for God as "father" when it literally means "daddy." It is a term of gentle, intimate affection and used only toward a very tender, indulgent, and warmly loving father. God is a father, all right, but he is also a mother. Occasionally Christians like the famous Juliana of Norwich referred to God as "our loving mother." It seems an awkward phrase to many of us, though it doubtless would please some of the people in the Women's Movement. But there is nothing wrong with the phrase. God is father and mother, mother and father; God is sister and brother, brother and sister; God is lover and spouse, spouse and lover. To put the matter in a more abstract way: All the attributes found in our own sex and in the opposite sex are combined in God.

So we can see the old Reformation argument about whether devotion to Mary took away from devotion to God completely missed the point. Mary isn't there as a rival of God; she is there as a "sacrament" of God. That is to say, Mary's role is to tell us something about God. Strictly speaking, we don't need Mary to know that God is gentle and loving and tender; but having a warm, beautiful, gracious, tender woman as a reflection of the tenderness of God makes it a lot easier for us to remember that there is material tenderness in God. We look at Mary holding Jesus in her arms in the crib scene and we should note very carefully that this lovely scene very powerfully conveys to us that God is gentle tenderness and cares for us the way a mother cares for a child. This is not rhetorical exaggeration; this is simple truth.

The old story was not all that wrong, although we would perhaps have to modernize it a bit and say that God himself would be the one to design ways to sneak us into heaven at the last minute when everything we did in our lives would seem to aim us in the opposite direction. The whole point of Mary in Christian devotion is to show us that we are dealing with a God who is tenderly and lovingly scheming to prevent us from escaping his seductive attractiveness. Does that kind of God scare us? Tenderness always scares us a bit because it strips away our pretenses, our defenses, our fakery and leaves us totally open to the one who is tender and loves us. This is always frightening. So if we are to be afraid of God, it should not be because he will send us to hell if we commit but a single mortal sin; rather we should fear him because there is no way to hide from his loving tenderness.

11
Mother's Love

During his all-too-brief September pastorate, Pope John Paul I said one day in a talk that the love of God was more like the love of a mother than the love of a father. There was horror and shock in many of the Italian newspapers. A number of writers were eager to explain that either there was no basic change in Christian doctrine or that there had been a basic change and that now there was a fourth person in the Blessed Trinity. In his next public homily the "smiling pope" laughed it all off by saying that he was only quoting the prophet Isaiah.

It may have been that Pope John Paul I was only repeating traditional doctrine. Nevertheless, the way he said it and the occasion on which he said it, in a simple public audience, was both shattering and effective. As William and Nancy McCready put it in an article several years ago, God is a mother, father, brother, sister, lover, friend. Every human love we know is but a reflection of God's love. Pope John Paul I who, it would seem, had a superb relationship with his mother, spoke of the maternal love of God, emphasizing thereby the maternal, affectionate, nurturing, supportive, binding-up-the-cut-finger-with-a-band-aid dimension of God's love. In a Catholic Christian religious tradition, the essential role of the Blessed Mother has been to manifest and reveal the maternal side of God. It is appropriate, to reflect on Mary, the "sacrament" (that is to say, the *revealing symbol*) of God's maternal love. God does indeed care for us the way a mother cares for a little baby, the way Mary cared for Jesus in Nazareth and Bethlehem. Despite all our fears, our failures, and our anxieties, we still believe in that tender, maternal side of God's love, in a smile something like that of Pope John Paul I's.

What do mothers do? They comfort you when you are sick, provide food, answer questions, take good care of you, and, more important than anything else, make sure that you know you're loved. Sometimes they are impatient, angry, sometimes they reprimand you or even punish you. But still, your mother is the woman who has carried you in her body for nine months, brought you into the world, protected you when you were a helpless infant, and the person who loves you more than anyone else in the world— at least in our culture where it is the mother who can most afford to show her affection for you. At best, mother's love is gentle, kind, tender, reassuring, comforting, free. That is the way Mary loved Jesus, that is the way God loves us.

It often doesn't seem that way. Each of us looks back and sees disappointment, heartache, failure, tragedy. If God loves us so much why does he permit these things to happen? Why did he permit John Paul I to die so soon? Why does he permit anyone to die? It is a strange kind of mother's love when God claims to love us as a mother and then lets us suffer and die. The answer we can give is that a little baby does not understand why its mother permits it to cry and suffer even though she assures the baby it is temporary and may even be for his or her own good, so we can never hope to understand God's designs for us. Indeed, the difference between a baby's intelligence and the mother's intelligence is minor compared to the difference between our intelligence and God's. It is the most difficult part of our faith to accept that a loving, maternal God can permit such apparently terrible tragedies. Though we are nonetheless committed to our faith, the joy that will come eventually will be so enormous that we will forget the suffering just as the baby forgets the five minutes of acute discomfort before the bottle is brought to him or her.

However, the point is not to explain the problem of suffering but rather to reassert our fàith. The love of Mary for Jesus which we see in the Christmas crib scene is a reflection of God's love for us. Indeed, God's maternal concern for us is even greater than that which Mary had for Jesus.

We honor Mary because she reflects God who has given birth to all of us and who renews our life constantly, promising us that eventually we will experience a life in which there will be only happiness and joy.

12
Divine and Human Love

Wedding days are times of joy and celebration. The man and woman have made their public commitment to one another and are possessed by the happy anticipation of the joy, the satisfaction, the pleasures, the sharing of life which is ahead of them. It may be that their expectations of happiness are unrealistic and superficial. They have no idea of the price they will have to pay to keep their love alive and to reap the full harvest of married joy. Superficial or not, they still must celebrate. The man who has just taken a bride would be a strange, unnatural man if he was gloomy, melancholy, grim faced, and somber on his wedding day. Similarly, the woman who has just taken a husband would be thought very strange if she was glum, depressed, unfriendly at the wedding banquet. Doubtless such things happen at marriages but when the guests see an unhappy groom and a glum bride they quickly conclude that there is something wrong with the marriage and that its chance of lasting is slender. If you don't celebrate on your wedding day then when are you going to celebrate?

The married couple will learn as the years pile up after their wedding that marriage, like most human activities, has its cycles of "ups" and "downs," good times and bad times, periods of affection and joy, periods of misunderstanding and conflict. After awhile, if they're truly wise, they will recognize the ebb and flow in their relationship as something natural and normal. The "down" times are not to be accepted lackadaisically but neither are they cause for panic. Marriage grows, for most people at any rate, both through conflict, or at least disappointment, and then reconciliation and rebirth. The beginning of a marriage is a time for celebration, the married couple learn; then the rekindling of love through reconciliation and rebirth is cause for even greater and richer celebration albeit more private because so much more intense. If the husband and wife who have just experienced the exhilarating breakthrough of reconciliation and renewed love are gloomy and somber, if they do not celebrate the intense joy that they feel from revitalization of their love then they would be very strange folk indeed.

The comparison of married love to love between God and his people, between Jesus and the church, is one of which the scriptures are very fond even if it scandalizes the puritans who have come after the scriptural era. Jesus told the puritans of his time that the followers of his heavenly Father are not sour-faced men and women because they know they are caught up in

a love affair with a passionate, demanding, wonderful lover. How could you possibly be sour
and grim if you believe that that's what life is all
about? How can you be moody and melancholy
if you really believe that the passionate joy of
married love is not something more intense but
rather something less intense than God's love
for you? Even when the followers of Jesus do fast
they fast with smiling faces and light hearts not
as gloomy, doomy puritans.

But, as with all love affairs, the relationship
between the individual person and the Heavenly
Lover has its ups and downs, its times of joys
and its times of discouragements, its times of fidelity and its times of infidelity. So we learn
through the despair of Hosea and his faithless
wife that the love commitment that God makes
to us is implacable. We may drift away from him
but he does not drift away from us. There is no
escaping from his love because there is no way
we can put him off, run away from him, anger
him so that he loses interest in us. The option,
the reconciliation and renewal is always there,
almost forced upon us every day. We who are
the followers of Jesus of Nazareth have two
causes to be men and women of celebration and
joy, not only that God loves us the way a bride
loves her husband or a groom his wife. We know
that the love is endlessly renewed through a life
of failure and reconciliation. If we are sour,

grim, somber, gloomy folk the only reason is that we really don't take the faith we profess that seriously.

There is, of course, a "feedback loop" between divine love and human love. If marriage is a hint of how God loves us, then the fact of God's implacable love for us provides us with the strength and the generosity, the patience and the courage to grow in our married love, particularly in those painful but also joyous moments when we seek reconciliation and renewal, when our love becomes more intense than it ever has been. If God is always ready to be reconciled to us then indeed we must always be ready to be reconciled to one another.

13
Interdependence

As much as we would like to think that we are independent, free-living, autonomous individuals, we are in fact all dependent upon many other people to survive physically and emotionally in the world. We are dependent on the farmers who raise our food, the merchandisers who distribute it, the cooks who prepare it, and the sanitation department that disposes of the remnants of it. If we stop to think, for example, of how much work goes into delivering the morning newspaper to our doorstep—the publishers, the editors, the reporters, the advertisers, the printers, distributors—we realize there are literally hundreds of people. The delivery of the morning paper is indeed a miracle of human ingenuity that would have dazzled most of our ancestors. We take it for granted. The morning paper is always there, isn't it? Indeed, we become furious when something interferes with our routine morning miracle.

Human interdependence, then, is something so obvious that it hardly needs to be pointed out. But it is also so commonplace that we take it for granted. The complex marvels of interdependence that are at the core of modern civilization hardly excite us at all anymore. Nor, unfortunately, does the amazing interdependence which is the human family, a thing that is not known anywhere else in physical creation—at least not on this planet. Admittedly, we have been at the business of depending upon one another in families for several million years longer than we have been at the interdependence of delivery of the daily paper. Yet we are often better at getting the paper delivered than we are at family affection and love. The reason is probably that delivering newspapers is easy compared to managing the subtle interdependence of family life.

Jesus adds an extra dimension, a deeper and richer perspective on human interdependence. If we are all linked together, we are, in the final analysis, linked together through him. We are all branches of the human race; he is the trunk that holds us all together. Without our tie to him the branches will fall off the trunk and the network of relationships will dissolve. What exactly does Jesus mean by that? Is he really claiming to be the one who holds families together? Is he really assuming responsibility for the miracle of production and distribution which is the daily newspaper delivery? The answer is yes. Jesus is the vine that holds all the leaves and branches together in two very important senses of the word.

First of all, the human race is held together by

God's love. We had to learn to cooperate with one another in order to evolve into being human. Our prehominoid ancestors learned cooperation before homo sapiens could appear. Learning cooperation and getting it encoded in our genes was the absolutely critical step in producing humankind. According to some scholars like Richard Leakey, it all began when we first developed the ability to share food with one another, an ability which did not exist in any other species save in very rudimentary form. This learning to cooperate and having it become not only part of our culture but part of our biology was the essential step in God's plan for our becoming human. It was God's love that made it possible for us to learn how to love one another, indeed to depend on that love for our survival. Jesus, as a revelation of God's love, merely confirms, validates, and reveals to us more sharply the nature of God's elaborate loving plan.

If, then, the interdependence and love that is essential for humankind to be human, came into existence as part of God's plan, the role of Jesus was not merely to confirm and renew the vision of that plan. It was also to show us how to develop it and perfect it, to persuade us that it was possible to push loving cooperation much further than we had been able to do, to give us the pattern and the paradigm for remaking, developing, perfecting the already God-given interdependence of all humankind. So when Jesus says to us that without him we can do nothing, he means two things: That human interdependence was created by his heavenly Father and that it was paradigmatically redeemed, reformed, remade by his example. Without God's creative plan, there would have been no human interdependence; without Jesus' renewing act, there would be no motivation, no paradigm, no practical possibility of plumbing the depths of the human capacity for cooperation and love. Both metaphysically and psychologically, then, it is surely true that we human beings can do nothing without God and without Jesus. Even the most simple kind of cooperation, the sort that brings the daily newspaper to our door, is rooted in a cooperative instinct that is part of human nature the way God created it.

God made us cooperative, social, indeed loving creatures; Jesus showed us how to practice that love by generous service of others. Being kind, patient, sympathetic, cooperative—especially with those who are closest to us and to whom we have the greatest obligation of love—is a built-in tendency of our personalities, though one which sometimes is too easy to resist and hard to implement in practice. Since we live in a world animated by the heavenly Father, no risk taken in the name of love, no vulnerability chanced for the strengthening of love will be unnoticed or in vain. Without Jesus we can do nothing; with his help, with his model, there is nothing in the way of love we cannot do.

14
Friends and Friendship

Jesus came to the world to tell his followers and, through them, the world, about his Father in heaven. He told them they could call the Father by the intimate term *Abba*—"Daddy or Papa." He told them that the Father was a passionate lover, an indulgent parent, a dedicated shepherd who would risk his life, a crazy farmer who paid people who had barely worked for a half hour, a king who desperately wanted guests at his party, and now, finally, in his farewell discourse to his apostles, he plays his last card: The Father is a friend. As the Father loved Jesus, so Jesus loves his disciples, and he does not call them servants, he calls them friends. The love of the Father for Jesus, the love of God for humankind is ultimately the love of friendship—the most noble, the most powerful, the most generous, the most sustained of human affections. Even between husband and wife sexual passion ebbs unless it is sustained by the deeper, stronger, richer ties of friendship.

Let us ponder the various friendships we have had during our lives. The children we played with in the streets or alleys as little kids, the classmates we walked to school with, the teenage crowd we hung around with, the intimate confidante with whom we shared our worries and/or fears as young adults, our spouse, the colleague or co-worker with whom we can relax, the teacher who provided us not only with knowledge and ideas but with excitement and challenge, the leader who inspired us and directed us—all of these human friendships, without which human life would not be possible, are sacraments; that is to say, they are revelations of the nature of the intimacy between God and us. "Is that what Jesus is talking about?" we ask, almost in disbelief. "Does he really claim to be a friend like that? Somebody we can talk to, somebody we can be at ease with, somebody with whom no pretense is required or even possible, someone to whom we can turn in trouble, someone who will share our joy, someone who understands us even better than we understand ourselves, somebody who is always there, rock-solid, when we need hope and encouragement, someone who is interested in our happiness and our welfare and who wants us to be the best that we are but still leaves us free to do that at our own pace? Is that what Jesus says religion is all about? And if it is, why do we permit ourselves to be afraid?"

At times the church seems to be beating us over the head with reassurance and encouragement. The Good Shepherd, the vine and the branches, the affection of Jesus laughing at his apostles as he eats the fish, the dream come true on Easter, and the description of God as a friend —passionate, committed, persevering, permanent. It is almost as though the church wants to stretch out the Easter joy as long as it possibly can to persuade us that everything will be all right. It will all work out, there is no need to worry; for, after all, is not Jesus our friend?

There are, of course, different kinds of friendship. Few of us have been able to sustain through a lifetime the friendships of our grammar school years. While there is always a special stirring of emotion when we encounter an old friend we have not seen for ages, other friendships come to an end—some abruptly, some even in conflict, and yet other friendships are so durable that nothing can sunder them whether it be distances of thousands of miles or separations that go on for years. So there are gradations of friendships, degrees of durability, of commitment, intensity, and involvement. If a marriage is also a friendship, then it becomes a relationship of incredible strength and power. Jesus tells us that he is our friend just the way that he and his Father are friends. This is a way of informing us that the most durable, the most powerful, the most intense of human friendships is only a bare hint of the kind of friendship Jesus and Father feel toward us. Think of our strongest, most passionate, most persevering friendship; then where the strength and power of that

friendship ends, the friendship of Jesus only begins. The invitation is that we should become
friends with one another just as Jesus is a friend
to us.

It is a mistake to think that Jesus wants us to
have an intense relationship with everyone.
There are rational and reasonable degrees of
friendship. When he invites us to be friends the
way he is a friend to us, he is talking not about
intensity but about generosity. We should strive
to be as generous in our various relationships,
according to the nature and limitations of those
relationships, as Jesus is with us. Generosity
with a colleague or co-worker is not the same as
generosity with a spouse. What Jesus has said, in
effect, is, "I am generous with you in my friendship; I want you to be appropriately generous in
the same way in all the friendships in your life."
The issue, then, is not so much extending a network of intimate relationships which would be
impossible for anyone to sustain, but intensifying appropriately the network of relationships
we already have. We respond to the invitation by
making our present relationships richer and
deeper, and in particular by intensifying the
depths of those most important and critical
friendships in our lives, the friendships with our
spouse, our children, our parents, the people
who are closest to us.

Friendships are to be treasured. They are

among the most wonderful gifts of our existence. To say that each of our friendships is a revelation, a secret hint of the friendship of Jesus for us, is not to downgrade our human relationships, not to turn them into pious tools; it is rather to upgrade them, to see them as part of a spectacular plan of love which animates the universe. It is Jesus, the greatest of our friends, who comes to us in all of our friendships, particularly in those friends who love us most deeply and whom we love most deeply.

15
Love and the Trinity

Human relationships don't stand still; they either grow or decline. Most close human relationships, marriage in particular, seem to go through cycles: affection, tenderness, responsiveness, then preoccupation, distraction, insensitivity, misunderstanding, quarrel, reconciliation, and beginning again. These things are normal enough; indeed they are means of growth and development of an intimate relationship so long as the ebb of the cycle does not become so low that there is not enough emotional energy left in the relationship to bring it back again. It is also the experience of those who are in close relationships that the energy of the relationship takes on after a while almost a reality of its own. It has its own dynamism, its own direction, its own power. Eventually, particularly in a marriage, the energy of the relationship becomes such a powerful reality that it almost seems distinct from the two partners. The husband and wife, in other words, are caught in their own love; and while the cycle may have been slowed, the love is so powerful that it is simply unthinkable that the relationship should break.

The Trinity is something like that. It is a network of relationships so powerful and so intense that the relationships themselves are personified and assume a reality of their own. Indeed, the relationships *are* Reality. Such an explanation does not make the Trinity any more "comprehensible," but it does afford us, when we find ourselves involved in, locked into, and sometimes even trapped in intense emotional relationships a feel for (though a very vague one) the energy and the dynamics that are at work in the internal relationships of God. God's knowledge and love are so powerful that they are personified, with knowledge being the Son, and the love generated from the knowledge of the Father and the Son being the Holy Spirit. God is a community, God is a network of relationships, God is not passive inactivity but dynamic energy, electrical currents, as it were, bouncing around from pole to pole. Unlike our human relationships, the ones in God do not have an ebb and flow; but in some way like our relationships, the Trinity is the dynamic energy of interacting love.

One would not have suspected this, though after learning about the Trinity one can see that it is reasonable enough. Of course, love is relational, communal, dynamic, energetic. It is an interesting and illuminating bit of information, though also stupifying, to learn that God is relational. But the doctrine of the Trinity has not been revealed to us either to stupify our imagination or dazzle our spirituality or inform our curiosity; it has been revealed to us to help us. We are told about the Trinity not to test our faith "under pain of mortal sin" but rather to be reassured that since God is relational, he is able to relate to us. Indeed, in some staggering way that gives us a headache when we try to figure it out, we are dealt into the relationships of the blessed Trinity.

We have been absorbed by the passionate love which is the Trinity and whose power and breadth and depth dwarfs the cosmos. All the exploding novae, all the expanding universes, all the deadly black holes are as nothing compared to the power of the internal love in the Trinity; and we have been let into the secret. More than that, as Jesus makes clear, we are sent forth to preach this love in this world in the name of the Trinity. We are messengers of love, revealing love in the name of love. More than that, we reveal that love precisely in and through our own loves. The more energetic, outgoing, dynamic, generous, passionate our love is, the more the love which is the Trinity is revealed to a world still trying to figure out whether the cosmos is ridiculous, absurd, capricious, vicious, or, just possibly, gentle and benign.

In Hebrew the word used frequently in the time before Jesus for the Holy Spirit was "Shekhinah." The "Shekhinah" was in earlier days merely "the Presence" of Yahweh. As time went on it became Yahweh's "Spirit," that is to say, Yahweh's love. In some mystical versions of Judaism between the two Testaments (versions which were something less than completely Orthodox) the Shekhinah became Yahweh's spouse. The Orthodox, rabbinic Judaism of the time of Jesus was properly afraid of the dangers of the fertility cults and ignored this mystical and popular component of the tradition—though Jesus himself described the love of his Father many times in ways that were anything but patriarchal.

The Holy Spirit's role in the New Testament is often characterized in ways that could be thought of as tender and maternal. One does not try to read back into the New Testament feminist concerns which were not there, yet it is certainly the case that the tradition out of which the doctrine of the Trinity emerged is indeed involved in a notion of the deity that is not only relational but also a relationship of persons alike yet different and tied to each other in passionate love. In the "pre-Trinitarian" thinking (at the time of Jesus, in other words), the relationship of the Trinity, like the relationship of Jesus and the church, was thought of as best reflected in human marital love.

16
Hunger for Love

It is Friday night, and you are invited to a dinner party. The time set for the party is 7:30. You are used to eating at 6:00 or 6:30, so the 7:30 starting time is a warning. Dinner is going to be late. You know that after some desultory drinking and munching of hors d'oeuvres dinner will be served two-and-a-half hours after it should be. Your appetite will be spoiled by the hors d'oeuvres, your head made woozy by the drinks. You arrive discreetly late only to find you're the first one there. By 9:00 o'clock the hostess acknowledges that dinner will be slightly late because some guests have been unavoidably detained. At 9:45 they finally show up, not even bothering to apologize. Of course, they have to have a drink too. Finally, at 10:00 you get to eat the overcooked vegetables, the soggy salad, and the overdone meat—three-and-a-half hours after civilized Americans have long since finished their dinners. You try to console yourself with the thought that maybe a little bit of purgatory has been removed from your account.

There are far worse hungers in the world than that induced by the late Friday night dinner party. Many people all over the world go to bed hungry at night, including some Americans. But for most of us the experience of physical hunger is limited to diets, juggled schedules, unexpected delays at the airport, and days when we are so busy we forget about eating. Unlike the other people in the world and unlike most of our ancestors, physical hunger is a rare experience for us. We don't fully appreciate the symbolism of the Eucharist as food. We understand, of course, the implications of gathering together around the table with those we love to share common life and to—at least on some nights, when the noise of the arguing isn't too loud—reinforce and strengthen our love. But the other experience that is involved in the Eucharist symbol—the desperate, hungry craving for food—is something we have experienced only rarely in life if ever.

We shudder with horror and shake our heads in astonishment at the story of the young people trapped in the plane crash in the Andes mountains who turned to cannibalism to stay alive. If such a decision was proper, according to the point of view of moral theology, we still cannot imagine what it is like to have been that hungry. The best experience of hunger we have is the one we impose on ourselves through diet, either because we are overweight or we are one of the few who still fast during Lent. We know what a marvelous feeling it is to permit ourselves a sliver of roast beef or a spoonful of ice cream after the diet or fast is over. The whole experience is of the increasing desire for food that we know we can't have. We are hungry for something we want, something that will bring us a bit of transient happiness; but as attractive as the piece of chocolate cake looks and as much as we want it, we simply can't have it.

A much more basic hunger is that for love. We want desperately to love and to be loved. The movies and the stories end with the hero and heroine loving each other and living happily ever after. They merely reflect how desperate is our hunger for perfect love. The comparison between our longing for love and our longing for food is especially apt. Without food we cannot live, we feel empty, dissatisfied, distracted, unhappy; similarly with love. The hunger for food may make us physically ill and put us in the hospital with malnutrition; the hunger for love makes us humanly and spiritually starved, and may eventually put us into a mental hospital. As St. Thomas Aquinas himself has said, humans are creatures who must either love or die.

Jesus chose the appearances of food to continue his presence here on earth both because the meal is that which brings together those who love one another and because, just as physical food satisfies the biological hungers of the human composite, so love satisfies the spiritual hunger. The perfect love of God as revealed in

Jesus satisfies those hungers completely. Until the time of fulfillment, those hungers are partially satisfied through our human loves by which God reveals himself to us. Jesus wanted to link the satisfaction of our hunger for love in God and its partial fulfillment through his presence among us on earth with the love we experience for those who sit around the table with us whether it be the Eucharistic banquet table at church or the banquet of friendship and love with those to whom we are close. The Eucharist, then, only had meaning as a sacrament of love: God's love revealed through Jesus and human love deepened and enriched and strengthened by the presence of Jesus among us. The Eucharist is a sacrament that satisfies our hunger because it promised the fullness of God's love and it brings us together in friendship and affection to those with whom we are committed in love.

17

The Healing Power of Love

One of life's nicer experiences is having a headache go away. Oftentimes two aspirins will do it; or if it is the result of an infection, a few doses of antibiotics will effect a cure. What a relief when a new enzyme medicine dramatically improves the condition of a strained muscle or when cough medicine soothes a sore and rasping throat. Being injured or sick is no fun. None of us would seek sickness or injury simply because it is so nice to get well. However, when we are sick, the recovery experience makes life worth living again. Jesus came to heal sickness, sickness of the soul, but also, insofar as spirit and body are united in one person, some bodily sicknesses too. We Catholics do not reject the contribution of medicine to human health. Furthermore, we are skeptical of the claims of miraculous healers who allegedly cure physical ailments. Still, many of the troubles that afflict humankind are psychological or even spiritual in origin. While faith is no substitute for medical or psychological help, the other side of the coin is also true: medicine and psychology are no substitute for faith.

Jesus was a healer. Even agnostic historians who study the evidence concede that the tradition of Jesus as a healer is too strong to be dismissed as a creation of the early church. But the miracles of Jesus, as important as they are in the traditions about him, were not intended to be "proofs" that we could use in arguments against unbelievers. Jesus explicitly rejected the demands for such proofs from his own generation; but despite that rejection, later generations of Catholics have still tried to use miracles as proofs. Rather, the miracles must be thought of as "signs," that is to say, revelations of what Jesus was about rather than proof of who he was. This distinction is very important. Jesus did not cure to "prove" that he was the Messiah, the Son of God, a messenger of Yahweh, or anything of the sort; he worked miracles to reveal that God's love was healing and that he had come into the world to show us even more about the healing power of God's love.

God's healing love is primarily spiritual or human. It heals the separation between God and humankind, between humans (particularly those who love one another), and, finally, between humankind and the natural world. Insofar as the religious wounds from which we suffer also affect our bodies, God's healing love can improve physical health too. We know enough about psychosomatic medicine to know that there is an important spiritual dimension to much of human illness. If faith will not heal some illnesses by itself, it can nevertheless be a substantial help in healing many. Finally, it also seems to be the case that when we are psychologically, spiritually, humanly run down, we are much more likely to be prey to bodily affliction and illness than when our psychological and spiritual morale is good.

How does love heal? Its principal healing effect comes from its capacity to exclude fear, at least drive fear into retreat. When we are less afraid, the whole human person—spirit and flesh, body and soul—has an enhanced sense of well being. It functions more effectively. Fear is a human disease, not just a disease of the soul; and when love exorcises fear, it improves the well-being of the whole person not just the spirit. Catholics have very properly avoided the extreme emotionalism of some kinds of faith healing. But they should not go to the opposite extreme and think that the healing love revealed by God through Jesus is purely spiritual with no impact on the well-being of the rest of the human organism. God's love heals humankind—the totality of human nature and not just one part of it.

Note the gentleness with which Jesus heals— so much in contrast with that of many current faith healers (including a few Catholics who are now practicing that form of enthusiasm). He is kind, courteous, considerate, concerned about the woman's embarrassment and worried about the little girl's hunger. There is no denial in this healing power of God as revealed by Jesus of strains and conflict. For reasons that we do not understand, disease, sickness, accident are part of the human condition; so are quarrels, conflicts, misunderstandings, and enmities, as is tension between humans and their environment. Jesus does not explain why these things exist or promise that they will cease to exist. Rather, he reveals to us that they are all curable: the sickness of death can be conquered, humans can be reconciled with one another, and the relationship between humankind and environment can be one of respectful use and not exploitation. He shows us that all these are possible under ordinary circumstances—not by miraculous intervention but by love putting fear to rout. Fear sickens, damages, destroys; love reconciles, integrates, makes hopeful. Love, of course, requires risk, vulnerability, openness. To enter the vulnerability of reconciliation, of respectful use of nature, and of confidence despite worry, one needs to agree that finally one lives in a world where love is stronger than hate, life is stronger than death, goodness is stronger than evil.

We pay little attention, it is to be feared, to the role of Jesus as healer and to the healing dimensions of God's love, as well as to the multiple healings that God makes possible in the human condition. We should ask ourselves how much the physical symptoms we experience are really the result of fear and would go away if we believed in the power of God's healing love (remembering that faith and love cannot heal *every* ailment). And how many of the sicknesses, injuries, frailties in our human relationships would also go away if we believed in that healing love?

18

Love in Conflict

Is there a parish in the post-Vatican II American
Catholic church that has not been troubled by
factional conflict? Maybe there are a couple, but
not very many. Time after time after time, parish
councils, school boards, parish advisory committees, finance committees, and all the other
committees have emerged something like the
plague of seventeen-year locusts to occupy the
time and energy of clergy and parishioners alike
in explosions of disagreements, arguments, bitter quarrels and sometimes open conflict. We
are learning the hard, painful way what our
separated brothers have known for some time:
you democratize a local congregational struc-
ture and you ask for trouble. Unfortunately we
have yet to learn the skills many of our separated
brothers have acquired at minimizing conflict
and finding smooth, sensible, and, indeed,
Christian ways to resolve differences of opinion
without exploding into open combat.

Does this mean we should give up our parish
councils and school boards, our committees, our
discussions, our search for compromise and co-
alition within the parish community? Surely not,
though it does mean that the skills of local
democracy are not easy to come by and that we

must all be wary of that kind of person who gets his or her kicks out of being a wrecker of local parish committees and councils. It also means, and it is an especially important observation, that none of us is in a very good position to laugh at the apostles who made fools of themselves by their silly fights about who was going to be first in the kingdom of Jesus. They completely misunderstood what the kingdom was going to be. Surely our own fights in a parish setting are going to be equally ridiculous.

But our purpose is not so much to settle any of the ongoing battles which may trouble our parish communities. It is, rather, to suggest that there is a strong propensity in human nature to get into unnecessary fights. Conflicts, disagreements, working out misunderstanding, tension, and injustice is absolutely essential to any healthy human group. A husband and wife, for example, who claim they never fight are probably kidding themselves about the latent strains and tensions that exist in their marriage. It is much better to fight in the open about the things that trouble us than it is to keep them secret, to store up angers and aggravations, and then finally dump them on the other person after 20 years of waiting for the opportunity.

If it is a mistake to paper over real conflict situations with a phony piety, then it is equally a mistake to let the conflict situations get out of hand or exceed the appropriate proportion of the subject matter at issue. You would think a husband and wife were utterly crazy if they got into an argument that reduced their relationship to absolute silence for two weeks over a difference of opinion about breakfast foods (though one ought not to rule out the possibility that such conflicts do often occur). Similarly, the perennial arguments about what children should wear at First Communion, which go back in the memory of the American church until the memory of humankind runneth not to the contrary, are probably not worth the energy, the anger and the animosity that they generate. The sad truth about our human nature seems to be that a lot of us love conflict, and we stir up conflicts about small points because such arguments are either emotionally satisfying to us or provide ways for us to discharge our neurotic needs. The apostles' fight was clearly a foolish and frivolous argument, yet that didn't stop them. And it doesn't stop us from having fights over things as trivial and neurotic.

We can probably say even more. It is precisely those of us who have great big unresolved conflicts with our parents, our spouses, or our children, who are most likely to transfer those conflicts to other areas of our life. If we happen to be active in church affairs, then we transfer them to church committees; if we happen to be political activists, then we specialize in breaking up political groups into factions, spending more time fighting with one another than taking on the other party. We could almost take it as a rule of thumb that the people who are most likely to get into conflicts outside the family are those who have the most serious unresolved conflicts in the family. If the sons of Zebedee, for example, were especially pushy with the other apostles in seeking a high place in the kingdom of Jesus, the reason may well be that they had deep unresolved conflicts with their unquestionably pushy mother (who, we may surmise not unreasonably, probably also pushed around poor old Zebedee, too).

How did Jesus handle this silly quarrel among his followers? He reminded them that they had been brought together not to argue about power but to serve one another in charity and affection. It is about the only way you can deal with conflict within your community, though historically it has not always been a successful strategy. As far as we can gather, the apostles continued their petty fights despite the reminder from Jesus that they were being called to serve and not to be served, to help and assist one another, not to act as overlords toward one another. Jesus gave them the perfect example of how to behave toward those who are our close friends and loved ones, but the apostles don't seem to have spent much time trying to imitate Jesus in this matter. Again, before we laugh at the apostles or ridicule them, we might ask ourselves whether we are in fact any better.

Most of the petty resentments and rivalries which occur among groups of friends (or in families) are as ridiculous and as pointless as the apostles' argument about their relative positions in the kingdom of Jesus. In the name of intelligence, maturity, and common sense, as well as in the name of Christian charity, we ought to eliminate such foolishness from our lives. Today is as good a day as any to ask ourselves how many absurd, childish quarrels we have either caused or continued that were simply not worth the energy. Let us proceed to laugh at our own foolishness while we laugh at that of the apostles.

19

Sexual Love

Many Catholics can still remember the days when young folks attending retreats or religious instruction classes or Catholic high schools were warned that young women should not wear black patent leather shoes because of what they might reflect. They also should not drink coffee with a boy, because it might make him think of having breakfast in the morning after spending a night together. They should not even eat pizza together because that might remind the boy of a pillow. The patent leather shoe symbol has become famous. It is funny, perhaps, in retrospect, though such an approach to sexuality had a bad effect on many young people in one generation and was probably a good part of the reason why young people of the present generation have refused to take the church seriously in sexual matters.

Such a narrow approach to human sexuality is opposed to the Catholic tradition. It represents a heresy called Puritanism. Novelist Bruce Marshall described it as the quaint notion that the deity made a mistake in arranging for the mechanics of procreation. Even today, however, many Catholics find it hard to believe that sexual pleasure is good, virtuous, commendable, and meant to be enjoyed. All of us are aware, of course, of the power of sexual attraction. It begins very early in our existence, is dormant for a while, and becomes imperious and demanding when the adolescent years begin. It only ends, as Chicago's Cardinal Stritch once remarked, fifteen minutes after we're dead.

The purpose of sexuality is obviously to keep the human race going. As a number of scientists have pointed out in recent years the biology of human sex is strikingly different from that of our nearest relatives in the primate branch of creation. Such creatures as chimpanzees, baboons, and gorillas, who are closely related to us in their physical and biological structures, have completely different sex lives. Their sexual contacts are infrequent, hasty, with random partners, and completely lacking in anything like affection.

Human intercourse, on the other hand, is much more frequent (it can happen at any time of the month instead of just on a certain day or two), requires more time, seems to be much more pleasurable, and tends to create bonds of affection, however brief these may be. Sex is only occasionally on the minds of our ape relations, but for most humans it is almost always on their minds. In other words, these scientists say, humans are far more sexy than they need to be just to produce offspring.

They then propose an extremely interesting theory, which has important religious implications. Much of the intensity of the pleasure, the vividness of the imagination, and the permanency of our sexual preoccupation do not exist for reproductive purposes at all, but for creating a powerful bond between the human male and female, a bond which does not exist in our primate relatives. (Though it does exist—much more rigidly—in many other species, such as birds). The evolutionary purpose of such a bond, according to the scientists, is that given the long number of years required for a human infant to mature, it is biologically necessary for the parents to be intensely related to one another in order that they both might be present to protect and educate their child. According to such scholars, our prehuman ancestors had to develop an intense bond between male and female before the species was capable of evolving into homo sapiens. Intense sexual love, in other words, was a precondition for the emergence of humanity.

Those of us who believe in God would see in all of this a working out of the divine plan. We are intensely sexy creatures because such sexiness was required for us to become human. We are a little less than the angels, but we are the only animal creature who comes that close precisely because we are so highly sexed. It's the way God made us so that we could be a little less than the angels.

The vision of permanent and exclusive commitment that Jesus presents in the gospel is not to be thought of as an extrinsic rule arbitrarily imposed on us, but rather as a powerful propensity rooted in the evolutionary process that produced us. We are designed to be sexually loving beings (and celibacy is just another sublimated form of sexual love—a different kind of intense dedication).

If it is true that we are the most sexy of the higher primates, it is also true that in all too many human intimacies the powerful sexual attraction diminishes rapidly—mostly because the fears, the defenses, the risks, the petty angers, jealousies, vindictiveness which plague us all get in the way of the openness, vulnerability, tenderness, and affection which are necessary for the growth rather than the decline of sexual intimacy. The whole point is not so much that we *must* be faithfully committed to one another but that our passions and our love, particularly when they are reinforced by a vision of God's loving goodness so attracts us to our "mate" that we want nothing more but permanent and publicly committed fidelity.

20

Who Are the Saints?

The feast of all the saints was originally an attempt to Christianize Halloween. Paradoxical as
it may sound, All Hallows Eve came before the
Feast of All Hallows (saints). Halloween was not
known as "Halloween," of course; it had different names in different places in Europe. Its original name appears to have been "Samain," a Celtic feast which marked the passage from autumn
to winter, and was passed on by the Celtic people to those who came after them in Europe. In
the Celtic religion, all transitional times were
dangerous, but none more so than "Samain-
tide." For this was the time when all forces of
evil and death were released from the under-
world to celebrate the final death of nature and
the coming of the dead and gloomy season of
winter. The Christian churches, knowing that
the feast was too popular and powerful to eliminate completely, tried to divert attention from
demons to saints; but the peasant population
merely moved the demons back a day. The
church's later attempt to again divert the people
from their pagan past and their celebration of
the dead by instituting All Soul's Day did not
eliminate the residues of Samain. The haunts
and the ghouls and the walking dead are still

abroad on All Hallow's Eve, but now, quite benignly demanding "tricks or treats."

Most "trick-or-treaters" probably have not the slightest idea that they were the descendants, for a few hours, of frenzied and superstitious Celts— or rather, more precisely, the descendants of the spooks and demons, the ghouls and the ghosts, the haunts and the hobgoblins, the evil spirits and the "little people" who drove the ancient Celts to a last frenzy of fear before the dark days of winter. It is perhaps just as well. If they knew whom they represented, the trick-or-treaters might concoct some truly frightening tricks. Still, we might ask some of them the next day—as they recover from the mysterious stomach ailments that come from ingesting too many cookies and too much candy—if they had bumped into any saints on Halloween as they wandered around in the haunted mists. We might also ask them and ourselves, too, how one would know a saint if one met one.

All of us are saints in some fashion, because God loves all of us and destines all of us to eternal happiness with him. Only when we turn our backs on his love totally and completely do we cease to be saints. Yet there are people who are saints in a special way, and we do violence to the ordinary meaning of the word when we extend it today to cover all of us.

In the course of our lives we come to know

many good people. Of some we might even say, "That person is a saint." What do we mean? What is the identifying mark that tells us that a very good person might also be a saint? It is not just long-suffering patience though saints are usually very patient people; it is not the capacity to pray for substantial periods of time, though saints are generally pretty good at prayer; it is not kindness to other human beings, though your average saint is a paragon of kindness and sensitivity; it is surely not high-pressure sales-manship for the church or for religion, for, while saints believe intensely in religion and the church, they do not try to force their religion on others. What, then, is it that makes someone a saint?

What seems to distinguish saints from the rest of us is a certain kind of peace or serenity or tranquility or confidence. Saints suffer as much as the rest of us, maybe even more, because they are likely to be more sensitive; they rejoice like the rest of us, and maybe a little more, because they see more things in life that cause them joy. But whether it be suffering or joy, the saint has an implacable confidence in God's loving good-ness. Saints know that God's affection for us is so powerful that no matter what happens he will never let us go. Saints know that they are held in the palm of God's hand and that there is nothing to be afraid of since nothing ultimately or finally bad can ever happen to us.

The beatitudes praise the poor, the weak, the disenfranchised, the homeless not because there is anything in poverty or weakness that is good in itself but rather because the poor (in the New Testament sense, the landless peasant proletarians who lacked political power, economic resources, and religious sophistication) know that they cannot find security and wealth or power or religious influence in careful, minute observation of religious rules. The poor know that in this world security can be found only by clinging to the hand of God who loves us so much that he will never let us go.

It is easy to say that we all ought to live with such trust in God's love. It is even easy to assert that we do live that way. There are lots of people who go around telling us how much they trust God, but the God they seem to have in mind often looks more like a vice-president-in-charge-of-seeing-that-everything-goes-our-way rather than a lover who clings to our hand. It is very difficult, however, to realize that in fact we are all poor, all meek, all powerless, and that our dearly cherished security is nothing more than an illusion. The only difference between the saints and the rest of us is that they know the elaborate array of defensive securities that we have built up around ourselves are nothing but illusions.

In the days after the Second Vatican Council saints seemed to have temporarily gone out of fashion. Along with the Blessed Mother and other old-fashioned Catholic devotions, saints seemed, at the time, to be an embarrassing encumbrance in an ecumenical age. Then a lot of our Protestant brothers discovered saints, just as they had discovered Mary. Now we Catholics are in a hurry to catch up. We have discovered that saints are not plaster statues, not pious creeps, not impossible ideals, but rather models to encourage us, to reassure us that it is possible to lead lives in which one lovingly clings to God's hand, knowing that he will never let us down and never let us go.

21
Falling Out of Love

One out of every five Catholics who are married is now divorced, a divorce rate only slightly less than American Protestants but more than three times as high as that of American Jews. Leaving aside questions of the reasons for this increase in Catholic divorce and the family problems as well as the ministerial and pastoral problems associated with it, let us focus on the human anguish that such fractured marriages cause. Almost all of those divorced people once thought they were in love. They once walked down the aisle for a wedding mass or a wedding service blissfully happy, confident that they had discovered the secret of a joyous and fulfilling life (more or less). Now that enthusiastic affection and confidence have been replaced by anger, bitterness, pain, hatred, and disappointment. What went wrong? Were they really in love? Was their love an illusion? How can you tell the difference between love that will last and love that won't? Indeed, what is this much discussed but little understood emotion called love?

If God really is love, then we might be tempted to think that God is unreliable, unstable, unpredictable, because that's the way human love seems to be. We fall in love irrationally (though the irrationality only appears afterwards) and fall out of love often as quickly, if not nearly so painlessly, as we fall into love. But God tells us we should love him with our whole hearts, our whole minds, our whole souls. Then we should love our neighbor as ourself. God tells us this because he is inviting us to respond to a love that already exists in him for us. Is he not urging us to an emotion which is likely to get both us and him in trouble? God seems to be hinting that he has fallen in love with us and wants a response from us of our love. But we wonder, if God falls in love the way we humans do (or at least *like* the way we humans do), does he also fall out of love the way we humans do?

Love ends in some human relationships because there never really was love there to begin with. The personalities were so mismatched, the insensitivities so great, the immaturities so pervasive that the initial attraction was little more than childish infatuation. In many cases, however, the infatuation was mixed and blended with what, though not exactly love, was an affection like the beginnings of love. The tender plant had no chance to grow, however, never becoming the fierce and implacable affection which led the actor Alfred Lunt to say to his wife Lynn Fontanne, "Murder, yes, but divorce, never!"

It is fear which does in love, blights the young plant, and keeps it from becoming a sturdy tree.

Fear prevents the development of love given once and for all and the taking of the risk inherent in any total love commitment. To love, as a modern Jewish philosopher puts it, means to have enormous power, the power of one who is totally defenseless and trusts nevertheless. Few of us are willing to pay the price of being totally defenseless to encourage that kind of love. To be loved means to expose ourselves to the awesome power that comes from the total vulnerability of another person. Either as the lover or the beloved, or, more precisely, both in our role as the lover and the beloved, we expose ourself to the terrible danger of being hurt—indeed to the certainty of being hurt some of the time. It is a risk most of us are very reluctant to take.

We may not have much choice in the matter because in fact we are by our very existence as creatures more utterly helpless in the face of God's affection than any human lover could be. But still we weave and bob, dodge and duck, and try to persuade ourselves that there is an alternative to accepting God's love, that it is possible to live a life in which we do not love God with our whole mind, our whole heart, and our whole soul and love our neighbor as ourselves. It is, we tell ourselves, possible to love God some, indeed a lot, without loving him totally. But as experienced human lovers know with absolute clarity, there comes a time in every love relationship when it must become either total or wither and die. It is only when love becomes utterly helpless in the face of the other that it becomes utterly implacable and irrevocable. And that is very scary indeed.

We must not think of human love and divine love as being discontinuous. Loving God and loving neighbors are but different aspects of the same raw and demanding human emotion. To love God demands a passion as unbridled as the most intense human intimacy. God's love for us is as reckless and as challenging as the most exciting human affection. We are only kidding ourselves if we think that our love affair with God is a neat, orderly, predictable, and easily controllable relationship while a love affair with another human is just the opposite. Love is love no matter who the lover is.

There is another close connection between our love affair with God and our human love affairs. It may be possible to make a total commitment to another human being, a commitment in which we become utterly defenseless in our relationship with the other, and still not believe in an all-powerful and all-loving God. You can have a successful human love affair, in other words, and not be explicitly engaged in a divine love affair. But it helps. It is a lot easier to run the risks of being in the palm of the hand of another human being when we are confident that we are ut-

1 800 432-9553 Ext 10

terly and totally protected by being in the palm of God's hand. If it is safe to exist, it is safe to love; but it is very difficult to believe that it is safe to exist unless one also believes in God's love. Religion may be the answer to the divorce rate, but not in the sense that it heightens our moral responsibility and makes us feel more guilty about the faltering of love. Religion underpins human love because it teaches us that God's love makes it safe for us to take the risks involved in human love.

22
Assault on the Family

One hears much these days about the "assault on the family" or the "decline of the family." Divorce rates are up, marriage rates are down, birth rates seem to fluctuate but seem to be moving downward, conflicts between parents and children are apparently on the increase. In addition, there are a number of people—experts on family life, professors who teach courses on family life in colleges and universities, journalists who write about family problems, some of those in the feminist movement, and some family "counselors"—believe that the family (the "traditional" family) is finished. Most people marry, most people have children, most people even stay married; but the "trends," we are told, are running against the "traditional family." According to such experts, the ideal will soon be honored only by an old fashioned and out-of-date minority. The "assault on the family" will win because it is the wave of the future.

There surely is an assault on family values, but we must be clear about what is the essence of that assault, because those who wish to destroy the family are for equal rights for women, because they support the right of women to have careers of their own, because they are for greater equality in family decision making, because they believe that husbands as well as wives should participate in the rearing of the children does not mean that any of these goals is inimical to preserving the family values to which the church is committed. Pope John XXIII and Pope John Paul II made it clear that there is no necessary opposition between feminism and Catholic family values. The assault on the family is more subtle, more pernicious. For it denies, sometimes implicitly, sometimes explicitly (as with the arguments of radical feminists), the possibility of love between husband and wife, between parents and children.

No one denies that intimacy involves conflict. Mothers and daughters do fight; so do husbands and wives. The different members of the family have different perspectives because they have different personalities. (Hence the "conflict" between Jesus and his parents when he stayed in the temple in Jerusalem.) There are doubtless times when husbands, wives, and children are all persuaded that the relationships into which they have entered or from which they have come is a disastrous mistake. The "assault on the family," however, takes for granted that conflict, exploitation, and unhappiness are typical and pervasive in family relationships, and that love is so infrequent as to be exceptional, and for most husband-wife, parents-children relationships virtually impossible.

It is precisely on this issue that the church must profoundly disagree. The church believes that love is possible between human beings. Indeed, that is the only reason for the existence of the church, since that is the essence of the message of Jesus. The church also believes that love and conflict are not necessarily opposed to each other, and that love grows through the successful resolution of conflict in reconciliation rather than in the elimination of conflict. (The "conflict" between Jesus and his parents was resolved and they were reconciled with one another.) The church finally believes that we love not by building escape hatches into our relationships, not by tentative, cautious, hedged-in commitments, but by the total gift of ourself to another. As Jesus gave himself to us, so we must give ourselves to those whom we hope to love. The hedged-in commitment is guaranteed to be a self-fulfilling prophecy. Love qualified by provisions, restrictions, limitations, and exemptions is not love at all.

Obviously some women are exploited by their husbands and children (as are some men exploited by their wives and children). Obviously, too, there is some conflict and exploitation in every intimate relationship. Furthermore, those who are going to be married are well advised to work out in advance an initially-agreed upon set of values that will regulate a relationship, though they would surely be wrong to think they can anticipate and avoid all the difficulties and conflicts that are bound to arise in any close intimacy. Nevertheless the Catholic vision still believes that love is possible—and not merely to a tiny minority of people. It believes that while most of our love is imperfect, virtually all of our love is capable of growth. Exploitation will be avoided not by provisional and tentative commitments but rather by increase in the richness and the depth of a commitment which can discover the love that lies beyond discouragement, misunderstanding, and conflict.

The "assault on the family" is something we must reflect on not because all of us are likely to be directly affected by it but rather because the rest of the world will take seriously the Christian position that love is possible in marriage and family only if it sees love reflected in our family lives. The world does not get a chance to see Mary, Jesus and Joseph loving one another; it does get a chance to see us loving one another, and it will judge the truth of the church's belief that love is possible by whether they see not only the possibility but the actuality of love in our family lives.

23
The Eyes of Love

A wise man once said that when mystery leaves a marriage love will leave shortly thereafter. His idea, apparently, was that when our spouse stops being intriguing, fascinating, surprising, he or she is no longer very lovable. Once we think we know the other completely, understand his or her moods, insights, abilities, secrets, hopes, and fears so perfectly that there is nothing more to be known, then we will quickly lose interest. The man was wrong. There is no such thing as an uninteresting person; there is no human being who is not filled with surprises. If the other has ceased to be surprising, love will not disappear, it has already disappeared. If we do not perceive the wonder and fullness of the other person, it is because we have lost the eyes of love with which to see.

The eyes of love see things that no other pair of eyes can see. Far from being blind, love is more acute than ordinary sight. The eyes of love do not fantasize or imagine a reality that is not there—not, at least, after the first infatuation is over. Rather, the eyes of love see things that others may not see, realities that may be there only faintly. But when these realities are seen by the eyes of love, they become more real, even more visible to others. When what is wonderful in us but hidden is seen by someone who loves us, it becomes both less hidden and more wonderful.

The Wise Men came to Bethlehem to see Jesus, to learn his secret, to perceive the wonderfulness of his coming into the world, to understand the hidden mysteries that he represented. They did not, of course, see anything that was not already there. They saw Jesus differently from Mary, Joseph, and the shepherds, because they brought interests and backgrounds of their own to the scene. When the Wise Men saw in Jesus wonders and marvels that no one else had seen, that God was manifested through Jesus in a way that he had not previously been revealed, it became clear that God's wonders are effectively manifested to humankind only when humans actually perceive them. God's lovability is revealed, in other words, only when we perceive that lovability. Since God's instrument is his lovability, there are things about him that can only be perceived by each one of us. God's manifestation, his "epiphany" through Jesus, depends upon our perceptions—not only our perceptions as a species, but our perceptions as individuals. Mary, Joseph, the shepherds, the Wise Men, each one of us all have roles to play in perceiv·

ing the wonderful secrets and mysteries of God and remanifesting those secrets and mysteries to those we love.

If we think we know all there is to know about God, then we clearly no longer love him. If God has ceased to be a fascinating, intriguing secret to us, then he is not an important reality in our lives. If we are content with a few catechism answers memorized long ago, a couple of arguments picked up in college or high school textbooks, an assortment of old images (most of them not very attractive or appealing), then we have not even begun to know God. And that particular epiphany that God has designed especially for each one of us has not begun to occur in our lives. We are living off our "capital" of God-knowledge, amassed a long, long time ago. The Wise Men were eager to travel to Bethlehem so they could learn more about the mysteries of the universe. We are quite content to be stay-at-homes and stick-in-the-muds, not knowing much about these great mysteries and not particularly caring to know much about them, content with the dull, monotonous simplicities of everyday life. God? Who needs him?

So our own epiphany, in all likelihood, has only just begun. Even if it is a well developed one and we know God now far better than we did a few years ago, it can still grow. Indeed, knowing God has no upper limits. The Wise Men could have returned to Bethlehem time and time again, learning more from each visit. Like the Wise Men, we are invited to return time and time again to learn more about the beauties, the goodness, and the wonders of God. If it sounds like a dull invitation, something not nearly as interesting as the football bowl games, or the pro championships, then the problem is that we do not know God well enough to realize how exciting the prospect is of getting to know him better.

How do we get to know God? Only by studying him, and not by studying him in books (though there is nothing wrong with that either—it's just not enough). We know God through his revelations, and most of his revelations, in addition to those contained in the scriptures and the tradition, are through other creatures, other events, other things that exist. We learn about him through the light of a winter sunset, the marvels of a snowflake, the gold-speckled blackness of a silent night, the warmth of a smile lighting up a depressing gray morning, a fine mist of white over dirty gray slush, the warmth of a family dinner after a long, difficult ride home, an old friendship renewed, an old love rekindled, sunrise on an icy lake, reconciliation after a quarrel. In all these sacraments of daily life, God reveals his/her mysteries, his/her marvels, his/her wonders, his/her splendid secrets. If we do not see him/her, or hear him/her, or feel him/her, the fault is not God's but ours.

24
Making Love Last

Wedding banquets are peculiarly ambivalent affairs. Sometimes the tension at them is so thick you can cut it with a knife. You sense that the bride's parents don't like the groom and the groom's parents don't like the bride. Both sets of parents also don't like each other. One or the other of the partners, and maybe both, seems less than enthusiastic about what is going on, but caught up in the inevitable social process there is no way out for either of them. Many of the close friends of the couple are not too cheerful; they've got their fingers crossed about what's going on, too. Such weddings are more like wakes than celebrations, and you wonder whether it will take even a year to put the couple in the divorce courts or the annulment tribunal.

Sometimes, of course, that's what happens. The reactions of friends and family are often the best reality check a couple can have. But occasionally, a quarter century later, you attend the anniversary celebration of the couple and marvel to note that they seem quite happy. They are still clearly very much in love with one another and take a special delight on their 25th anniversary day in proving the prognosticators wrong. You wonder how many fights and reconciliations there were, how much strain and conflict, and also how much intense love has kept these two seemingly mismatched people together so long. Indeed, despite all the troubles they must have had, they express joy and pleasure in their life together. The union between a man and a woman, you tell yourself, is an endless mystery.

The gospel story of the marriage feast at Cana has many different meanings, but the church emphasizes the parallel between God's passionate love and passionate human love. It suggests to us that the presence of Jesus at a banquet celebrating the beginning of the sexual union between the bride and the groom endorses forever the validity of the parallelism of human sexual intimacy and God's intimacy with the people he loves.

There are really two different elements in the sexual comparison of God's love for humans to that between husband and wife. First of all, the intensity of sexual union reflects the intensity of God's love for us and of our love for God when and if we get around to responding. Secondly, human sexualism is inconsistent, unpredictable —at times rewarding and at times enormously frustrating. Romance comes and goes. Man and woman are alternately deeply in love with one another and bored with the routine of their relationship. They learn very quickly that they have to work hard, pay close attention and be very sensitive if they are to sustain the intensity of their relationship. Care, attention, sacrifice, endless reconciliation are the price of marital fulfillment.

These are the parallels between human passion and divine passion. Not only are they both intense, but both have ups and downs, and both, to be successful, require dedication, effort, and frequent reconciliation. There are two conclusions we must draw from the use of marriage imagery in the Scripture. First of all, the more intense the passion between husband and wife, the better "sacrament" they are; that is to say, the better they reflect the love between God and the church. Despite all the puritanism we may have been taught, despite all the inhibitions that may have been pounded into us when we were young, this assertion is unassailably true, and the efforts of husband and wife to grow in affection through the course of their marriage are efforts dedicated toward a more effective sacrament.

The second conclusion is the need for mutual relationship between reconciliation in marriage and reconciliation with God. The joy and happiness that comes to a married couple, which frequently heightens the intensity of their affection, when they have reconciled after a quarrel is a revelation of the joy that is possible when we are reconciled with God in renewing our love commitment to him. And because we are committed as Christians to the belief in God's passionately reconciling love for us, we are able to take the risks necessary to be reconciling in human love and to commit ourselves to intensifying the affection we have for those humans we love. Marital love, in other words, reveals God's love, and God's love strengthens our commitment and our courage to intensify our human love.

All of this is scandalous to the puritans and the Manicheans. But it should be pointed out that Jesus went to a marriage feast in Cana and saved that celebration of sexual union from becoming a disappointing failure. He also made marriage a sacrament. If it were not for human sexual attraction, if it were not for the fact that the human race renews itself through sexual differentiation, there would be no need for marriage, much less to make marriage a sacrament.

The challenge of the Cana story is obvious: married people must ask whether the intensity of their affection really does reflect the intensity of God's love, and whether their belief in a loving God has provided them with the motivation they need for growing in their sexual affection. These are disturbing questions for any married couple to hear, and especially disturbing to hear them in church. Yet if they were not the kind of questions the church should raise, Jesus would never have gone to Cana, and, at his mother's request, changed the water into wine.

25

Loving and Forgiving

Imagine that you are a parent and have gone out for the evening, leaving the baby sitter in charge of a couple of small children. You return to find the baby sitter in tears. The children have destroyed all the dishes in the house, smashed in the television screen, smeared the walls with crayons, and have begun to carve up the living room furniture with a knife. The kids say, "Gee, we're sorry. We won't do it again." You say in response, "Hey, that's great. We're really glad to hear you're sorry. Let's have a party to celebrate your sorrow and the lesson you've learned tonight." The baby sitter would never come back, of course, and the kids would begin to connive about the depredations they would work the next time you went out for the evening. If you acted that way with your children, not only would you be spoiling them rotten, you would absolutely be asking for more trouble—and you would most assuredly get it. If we reflect on this fact, we will have no doubt at all that Jesus is trying to do something in the parable of the Prodigal Son besides provide us with a pattern for child-rearing. Indeed, as all the parents in the congregation undoubtedly suspect, child-rearing isn't the issue.

It is easy to sentimentalize the story, to get lost in the pathos of the reunion between father and son. It is also easy to allegorize it, assigning to all of one's enemies the role of the other son. However, the parable is neither sentimental nor allegorical. The father of the story, quite candidly, is a fool. He is not taken in by his son's dubious sincerity; he doesn't even bother to listen to the mostly insincere speech the young man has prepared; nor would any parent other than a foolish one deal so unfairly with the other son, whose complaint is perfectly reasonable. Why celebrate disloyalty and ignore loyalty? Again, any parent who would behave that way would lose the devotion and respect of his children, because they might quite legitimately argue that if the only way to get attention is to be profligate, then why not be profligate?

Is Jesus celebrating folly? Is he urging parents to spoil their children? What is he up to in this parable? What is the point of the foolish, self-indulgent father, waiting on the porch and looking down the road, wondering whether the wandering son might return today? The parable is indeed about folly, the folly of God; and the point of the parable is utterly simple: God's love is so outrageous, so involved, so deeply committed, so passionately forgiving that by human standards it is foolish, almost lunatic. No human parent could possibly afford to be so indulgent and so foolish with his children as God is with us. That is quite literally what Jesus meant.

The parable is about God's love, his passionate attachment to us. Jesus' "instinct" about that love is that it is wild, bizarre, indulgent, forgiving and, indeed, ultimately foolish according to human standards. God can afford to be a lunatic in his love affairs, because he is God. We may find this approach to God to be disconcerting. How dare anyone say that God is a fool? But that is precisely what Jesus is saying. Jesus' claim to have special and unique knowledge about the father in heaven is especially and powerfully revealed in the parables of Jesus, where we come into direct and immediate contact with both the thought of Jesus and, more important, his religious vision, a vision which is profoundly disconcerting because Jesus was often, indeed almost always, reckless in his use of language. He was as reckless as he claimed God to be in his love. The beginning of the parable is utterly simple: God's love is foolish. Such a message may upset or disturb us, or it may make us think, or it may, in addition to these things, accomplish what Jesus had in mind—manifest to us how totally, completely, indeed wildly and passionately God loves us. Human lovers who act like God, Jesus says, would be locked up in an asylum.

The Prodigal Son parable is one of the classic

parables of Jesus. It has also suffered classical treatment, that is to say, people have tried to fudge its meaning, obscure its disconcerting twist, sentimentalize it, allegorize it, and hide its bitingly simple point. We don't like to hear God called a fool, much less an indulgent fool. Okay, so we don't like it, but it is still what Jesus is saying; it is his experience of the father's love. The very essence of Jesus' gospel and his religious vision is that God loves us with a wild passion which, if found in humans, would be interpreted as a sign of madness. No wonder the gospel so often seems too good to be true. Does Jesus really expect us to believe that? The answer is that he most certainly does.

The first conclusion that we must revel in and relish is the fact of our forgiveness. God asked so very little. The sincerity of the prodigal is dubious at best, but he made a move in the direction of the father and that was enough. The father overwhelmed him with love and would keep him by the sheer force of his affection. So it is with God. He demands a response from us, but his love is so great that even the most imperfect and badly flawed response is enough for him to bring out the garments and begin the celebration. The second conclusion is that while the behavior of the loving father in the parable is not a paradigm to be exactly imitated in child-rearing, it does provide a pattern for forgiveness, and the name of the pattern is generosity. Because we are limited creatures, we may not be able to be quite as wild as God with our forgiveness, but at least we should try to be generous. As we review our own generosity we should ask ourselves, where might it best be applied, especially in giving and asking forgiveness of those we love the most?

26

As We Really Are

We go through our lives covering up, hedging, dodging, dissimulating, deceiving. We engage in these behaviors not because we enjoy it but because it seems we have no choice. We cannot take the risk of being transformed, of letting others know us as we really are, because if they do so, they might see through us and we would cease to exist. We manage our self-revelation in tiny doses, keeping secret as much as we can, and revealing only the little we have to reveal in order to survive. When we hear the Good Shepherd say that he *knows* us, we ought to be properly terrified, if we understand what he is saying. How could it be that he knows us for what we are and yet we still live?

Self-rejection and self-hatred are as universal as original sin. Indeed, they are some of the primary consequences of original sin because they are rooted in the fear of non-being, which is at the heart of our fatal human flaw. Only a few of us have experienced in life the kind of love that makes us sufficiently secure that we don't have to hide or pretend. God may know us as we really are, we tell ourselves confidently, but we don't have to live with God every day. His knowledge may affect us at the end of our lives or at the end of the world, but he will not humiliate, ridicule, and embarrass us because of inadequacy now. So we spend much of our time and energy covering up these presumed inadequacies and trying to pretend we are someone we are not. It may also be the case that God loves us not only despite what we are but because of what we are. That may be fine for God; he's a very sympathetic and forgiving person. But all humans aren't that way. We can afford to be open with God, we can't afford to be open with our fellow humans.

The ridiculous part of the hiding, pretending, dodging game is that the person whom God loves is usually far more lovable than the person we pretend to be. That person of which we are ashamed, in other words, is a far more admirable self than the one which we fake out of our curious conviction that no one, save possibly a doting parent, could love the self we try to hide. It is even more ironic, of course, because generally we are not able to deceive those who love us. They do not love the disguises, the masks, the ducking and dodging games we play; they love the hidden self we occasionally reveal who intrigues, delights, and fascinates them. It is a savagely ironic business. Most of us are loved precisely because of that aspect of our personalities that we think the most worthless, the most unlovable, the most ridiculous, the most shame-

ful. God's taste, it turns out, and the taste of
those who love us is better than our own.

The Good Shepherd's claim to know us as we
are is actually a claim to much more than factual
information. The Good Shepherd is not into the
personality-type, psychotherapeutic, diagnostic,
test-score game. His knowledge implies and involves love. More precisely, his knowledge is the
kind of knowledge that comes through love. Because the Good Shepherd sees us through the
eyes of love, his knowledge is that of the old
scriptural sense of the word "know" when it is
used as a euphemism for sexual intercourse—"to
know completely and totally." The Good Shepherd, in other words, claims knowledge of us in
a way even more intimate than lovers have
knowledge of each other's bodies, more intimate
and more affectionate.

But even in our most powerful and intimate
human love the mutual game of dodging and
ducking not only survives but becomes an intricate and complex dance in which two people
share their bodies, share their lives, share their
home and children but still hide from one another for fear that if they become "transparent"
to one another they will be destroyed. And all
the while, of course, each is in love with precisely that aspect of the other which he or she is
most likely to want to hide. Rarely if ever does

anyone say to himself or herself in effect, "What does it matter. If I am known that well by God, and if the other person really sees through much of my elaborate dancing and game-playing, why not stop it. Why not make the leap of trust and stop pretending to be someone I'm not." Such leaps of trust have to be renewed constantly, and each time at the risk of pain and suffering. The alternative, however, is to build up stronger, thicker, more impassable walls of self-protection to isolate ourselves in a one-person unit where we are utterly and completely alone. The sociopathic personality does just that. While few of us are sociopaths, all of us know the temptation: we don't really believe that there is enough worth, dignity, or value in who we are to take the risk of entrusting our self to others.

There is a form of psychological game-playing that is especially common among those who have been through the pseudotherapeutic techniques popular during the "me decade" in which we use phony self-revelation as an elaborate technique for both hiding the self and punishing the other. We beat the other person over the head with self-disclosure, most of which doesn't disclose but actually hides the self even more. Such trickery, not completely uncommon among Catholics, is pernicious precisely because the people who engage in it deceive no one but themselves, and they deceive themselves spectacularly. It is the revelation of a timid soul who shares with us, sometimes brutally and painfully, a self which does not exist and has never existed, a self which all who love him or her—the Good Shepherd included—completely repudiate.

27

The Demands of Love

There was a time when films dealt with people falling in love. In our era of cynicism, however, we more frequently see movies about people falling out of love. Such efforts as *Kramer vs. Kramer, Starting Over,* and *An Unmarried Woman* are examples. They may or may not be clinically interesting. Falling out of love, heaven knows, is a frequent enough experience, particularly at a time when the commitment to persist in love is not taken all that seriously. Yet most of us still enjoy love stories more than unlove stories. The whole world loves a lover, as the cliche puts it, whether the lover is a young person in the giddy excitement of his or her first romance or someone who is blissfully celebrating a 50th wedding anniversary.

When Jesus bids farewell to his followers in the gospel, he is betting on the attractiveness of love to keep his work alive and to spread the community of his followers. He knows that love is irresistible. It was his own love for the Father, and that reflected in his love for those who came to him, that won for Jesus the sturdy little band of followers to whom he speaks. And while their own love for one another is badly flawed, he still urges them to concentrate on their love for one another as the most effective means they have for preaching the gospel. All their words, all their deeds, all their brave missionary journeys, all their sufferings, even their martyrdom will have little effect on a skeptical, cynical world if they don't love one another.

If Christianity has been somewhat less than successful in attaining the goals that Jesus laid down for his followers, the explanation is that all too often we Christians have been willing to try just about everything to spread the gospel except the love that Jesus demanded we have for each other. We have used high-pressure propaganda, hard-sell marketing techniques, threats of damnation, military force, even bribery and torture. How many times those to whom we have preached the gospel were able to really know us as followers of Jesus by the kind of love we had for one another is surely problematic. We have not taken seriously the message of the gospel, in part because we really didn't think Jesus seriously meant it, in part because we are dubious about the effectiveness of love as an evangelization technique, but mostly because loving one another is just too difficult. We tried to short-circuit the evangelizing process and substitute for love of one another the hard sell, because while we all know the attractiveness of lovers, we also know the enormous demands that love makes.

The loud, violent, and frequently bloody conflicts between those who claim to be the followers of Jesus have undoubtedly been the greatest barriers to the spread of his good news. Those who have watched and listened to us can quite properly say, "I thought we would know the followers of Jesus by their love for one another. Where is the love among these snarling, shouting, ranting, self-righteous, hypocritical Christians? Yet most people, at least in our environment, do not know the church through its teachers, its leaders, the pope, bishops, or even the parish priests. They know it through the Christians who are their neighbors. They will see the love of Jesus reflected, if they see it reflected at all, in the family life of Christians. The love of husband and wife for each other, of parents and children for each other, is, whether we like it or not, the principal evangelization technique we have available. It is precisely in our family lives that most of our neighbors know whether or not we are followers of Jesus of Nazareth.

If we are patient, sympathetic and understanding with our children (or with our parents) and more generous, more gentle, more healing, and more authentically affectionate with our husband or wife, then those around us will begin to wonder why. Eventually it will occur to them that the only possible explanation for the more intense love in our household is that we are followers of Jesus of Nazareth. The attractiveness of love is as irresistible to them as to everyone else. If our love is abrupt, exploitive, ill-tempered, thoughtless, and erratic and we still claim to be followers of Jesus of Nazareth, then our neighbors might be excused for wondering whether our faith ought to be taken seriously.

Members of Catholic families might well argue that it is not fair to put such an obligation on them. Why should their love be different from anyone else's love? Are they supposed to be some kind of superpersons? The answer that would come from Jesus is the gospel. If we have experienced the love of God as it has been revealed to us in the life, death, and resurrection of Jesus, then our human love may not be easy, but we have more powerful motivation and greater security in those loves. To be truly attractive, love must be giving, surrendering, serving, risk-taking. In the glowing light of the risen Jesus and the firebomb of God's love as manifested in the resurrection, Christians know that it is safe to take risks, safe to yield, safe to surrender, safe to give oneself in loving service. We love more fiercely and more intensely not because we are better people, not even because we are braver people, but because we are people who feel more secure. We know we have been enveloped by God's love. It is that we have understood that if the heavenly Father clings to us as he did to Jesus, indeed so vigorously that death could not contain him, then the risks of loving are not nearly as great as they seem. The joyous love that others ought to see in our family life is the joyous love to be found among those who know it is safe to take the risks of love.

28

God Our Mother

The Band-Aid is one of the most wonderful inventions human ingenuity has created. Consider the enormous improvement in the life of mothers that the Band-Aid has made possible. A child is cruelly assaulted by a sidewalk. Mind you, there is only a slight abrasion which will probably be gone by morning. But the small one's dignity has been offended and only maternal affection will heal either wound. A hug, a kiss, a swiftly applied Band-Aid, and the "owie" is gone. If the family supply of Band-Aids should be exhausted—well. . . . How could a Mom possibly love her children and be concerned about their "owies," if she permits the medicine cabinet to be emptied of Band-Aids?

The Holy Spirit, whom Jesus promises to send represents God's affection, God's tenderness, God's reassuring and loving care, God's maternal protection, God's commitment to healing our "owies"; indeed, God's willingness, to stretch the point a bit, to slap Band-Aids on our personality. The Paraclete, the consoler, the advocate, the loving protector and caretaker represents a strong strain of femininity that was always present in Yahweh in the Old Testament and which in the New Testament is reflected especially through Mary the Mother of Jesus.

In God, those characteristics and traits which we think of as separated according to gender in humans, are combined. God is both tender and strong, both ordering and loving, both aggressive and compassionate, both sensitive and vigorous, both pursuing and attracting. Catholic teachers speak of the "coincidence of opposites" by which they mean the blending of all the different characteristics that seem opposed in our human experience into one uninterrupted, smooth, divine perfection. It may seem strange to speak of God as a loving mother as well as a vigorous, challenging father. As noted, some saints, such as Juliana of Norwich, have referred to God the Mother; but ordinary Christians seem to have no problem of thinking of God that way. Fully one-third of the Catholics under 30 in the United States, according to recent research, think of God as a mother. (Young men are no less likely than young women to think of her that way). In most religions, the masculinity and the femininity of God are separated into male and female deities. The Lord Yahweh, God the Father, God the Mother, is above such distinctions. In him all perfections are combined without limitation, without boundary, without differentiation. Yet it is good for us to be reminded, insofar as he attracts and insofar as he calls, insofar as he cares for, protects, consoles, and heals, God is engaged in the kind of behavior that we humans tend to identify with mothers (though fathers who are truly strong are also able to do the same thing). It is interesting to realize that in Jewish folklore and in popular religious traditions, God's "Holy Spirit" had, if not a feminine identity, at least certain feminine aspects and residues in his/her identity.

In the older folk religion of the Jews, recent scholars have discovered, the "Shekinah" or "Holy Spirit" of Yahweh was indeed Yahweh's consort, his spouse. Even in some of the temple and synagogue worship that went on in big cities like Alexandria during the Diaspora, this concept of Yahweh was very much present. However, in the strict prophetic and later rabbinic Judaism of Palestine no such concept was tolerated, because Yahweh was considered to be utterly transcendent and hence far above and beyond such things as sexual differentiation. Traces and strains of the folk religion persisted, and the Shekinah, or Holy Spirit of Yahweh, which was embedded in the books of the Jewish scriptures as Yahweh's "presence" (that is, his loving and compassionate care), retained many of the maternal characteristics of the pre-prophetic and folk religion mother goddess. The point of all this is not that the prophets were wrong in insisting on the transcendence of Yahweh. On the contrary, they were perfectly right. The point, rather, is that the human insight that God is both maternal and paternal is virtually irresistible.

Undoubtedly our rediscovery of the maternal nature of God has been influenced by recent social and cultural developments. Something like this might not have occurred to anyone 15 to 20 years ago. But the rediscovery is not a twisting of the evidence to fit current fashion. It is understanding more clearly the deep and powerful strains in our heritage that have always been present. If one-quarter of the Catholic young people think sometimes of God as a mother, the reason surely is not sermons they have heard about the femininity of God or the maternity of God, but rather basic and fundamental religious instincts that reveal to them the loving tenderness, as well as the ordering power and strength of God.

To put the matter somewhat differently, we have always known that the Holy Spirit was the consoler, the protector, the advocate. Now we see that both historically and psychologically there are grounds for saying that these roles of the Spirit are based on the fact that God is both father and mother, husband and wife, the creative law-giver and the beckoning lover. Contemporary cultural development, in other words, enables us to see more clearly an aspect of the heritage that was always there but not always perceived quite so clearly. In fact, what Jesus said to the apostles is that he is going to leave behind a tender lover who will challenge us, take care of us, call forth from us that which is unique and most especially ourselves. It would not be wrong to see in the affectionate farewell of Jesus to his followers something that roughly parallels a father's going forth on a long journey, assuring his children that mother will take care of them in his absence, and that they will be truly loved and well protected while he is gone.

29

God Is Love

The movie *Kramer vs. Kramer* was certainly one of the hits of the 70s. It was well written, well directed, well acted, and it seemed to touch many people's lives as a plausible story of the three-cornered relationship of a mother, a father, and a son and the impact of divorce on that relationship. Not all human love relationships end as unhappily as the Kramer marriage did. Not all mothers and fathers end up fighting for the custody of their children, and most children are not caught in a situation where a court has to decide whether the mother or the father will have custody. But wherever there is human love there is conflict, and in the mother-father-child triad there is intense joy, great pleasure, and enormous conflict.

Few of us need to be told that the picture of love in such song words as moon, June, croon, and spoon is highly misleading. Love is not hearts and flowers, the silly sweetness of Valentine's Day; it is not the simple and forever romance of a love song. Love, the canticle of Solomon tells us, is as stern as death, as relentless as a fire, as unstoppable as the raging waters of a flood. It is the demonic and potentially destructive power that humans use to tear apart their own lives and destroy the lives of others. Love is not sweet, pretty, nice, and good (though it may partake of all those characteristics); it is rather a devastating power that both attacks and repels, both unites and separates. At the end of *Kramer vs. Kramer* the couple is still divorced, the man still has custody of the boy. Both have done enormous injury to the other and to the child, and yet they are still capable of powerful attraction for each other. One wonders, as the elevator door slams shut, whether that attraction will be resistible.

If love is such a devastating, overwhelming, and uncontrollable energy, why do we attribute it to God? Why do we say that God is love? Why do we think that it would be a compliment to God to refer to him as love? The answer seems to be that love is the most powerful and most pleasurable emotional force that we know. To say that God is love is to say that he is enormous energy and unsurpassable pleasure, an irresistible force, unmatchable beauty. In effect we acknowledge that love is too big for us to control, and we assert, perhaps bravely, that it is not too big for God to control. The enormous ambiguity and ambivalence of love, demonstrated in *Kramer vs. Kramer,* results not from the fact that love is evil but rather from our inability to control the energy, the power, the force, and the beauty of love.

The revelation about God contained in the doctrine of the Holy Trinity is that God is a loving community, that triadic relationships in our families are a vague and imperfect hint of the communal relationships in God. The energy, the force, the drive, and the beauty, as well as the passion and the power that exist in the human community—particularly the human familial community—also exists in a much different, much greater way, of course, in the community that is God. That human energy which we imagine being most like the energy that binds together the Holy Trinity is the energy of human love. God is held together as a community of three persons by a force, a power, a passion, and a beauty which is something like the force which holds together human lovers, human parents and children.

What does the Trinity then tell us in a practical way about our own loves? First of all, it tells us that we should not be surprised or overwhelmed by the raw power of love. Nor should we deny or repress the anger which is often the reverse side of love. Anger is both a protection against the one we love and also a demand that the other give up the protections he or she has built against us. Anger is love demanding union and love fearing union. It can destroy a relationship, or almost destroy it, as it did in *Kramer vs. Kramer*, but it can also clear away the obstacles to growth in the relationship. If you remember the film, one of the problems that led to the divorce was that the woman was not able to express her anger, and when she tried to, her husband was not able to listen. The question is not whether we are angry at those we love—of course we are, because love relationships are too important and too intense not to generate anger. Rather, the question is whether we are able to learn the skills of turning anger to constructive purposes.

The second lesson of the Trinity as a model and guarantee of love is generosity. The Father and the Son give themselves to each other totally, and that gift becomes the third person, the Holy Spirit. Without generosity there can be no love. The quality of generosity is finally the determinant of the quality of love. Our generosity cannot be total, like that in the Trinity, because we are limited; and it certainly should not be the generosity of the all-absorbing, never protesting doormat. But if we ever give up on trying to improve our skills at being generous to the ones we love, then our intimacy is in trouble. The excitement, the adventure, the pleasure and the fun will slip out of it; and energies which can be either creative or destructive, but not something in between, will almost certainly turn destructive.

One Catholic married man remarked, apropos of the church's frequent comments on "unbridled" passion: "For most of us, the problem is really "bridled passion." We stifle, in other words, the love energies within our relationships by the routine and monotony of everyday life. And we do so precisely because we are afraid of the power of such energies. Surely that was one of the things that had gone wrong with the Kramer marriage. We should ask ourselves whether we have not suppressed the passion of our love energies and by so doing turned them into potentially destructive forces in our family lives.

30

Keeping Our Commitments

None of the critical experiences of life are logical. What we want to be, where we want to live, whom we are going to marry, even the political candidate we are going to choose in an election, demands decisions of us that go beyond logic, beyond reason, demanding not just agreement or assent, which is fairly easy to give, but commitment, which, more than just an intellectual nod of the head, is an embrace of an object, a goal, by the entire personality. Falling in love with another human being, for example, and then deciding to marry that person is a non-rational, non-logical, non-intellectual process. Our minds may tell us that it is a wise and sensible choice, and we may ponder it very carefully before we make it. But in the final analysis the commitment of love to another person is a leap in the dark beyond the rational.

Why do we fall in love? That is a question which the philosophers, the poets, the storytellers, and the songwriters have asked for ages and have not been able to satisfactorily answer. Obviously there are many different persons that each of us might love. It is not unusual to be in love many times before our definitive commitment is made. Still, whether it is a shallow teenage crush or a mature, permanent commitment, love seems to transcend intellectual analysis. One answer is that we fall in love because we cannot do without the other person, we cannot tolerate a life in which the other is not near to us, we cannot bear a life in which the other is not part of our life. Another person comes to play this role for us because that other person is enormously attractive, though what makes him or her attractive differs so much with different humans that it is very difficult to isolate a pattern. Finally it comes to the fact that the other is simply nice to be with, compellingly and overpoweringly nice to be with.

Note that this is precisely how the followers of Jesus respond to him in the gospel of Luke. They discuss the intellectual evidence—who some people say Jesus is, who others say he is. But then, when he asks them who they think he is, there comes the definitive commitment, the leap of faith, the act of love. They believe in Jesus because they love him and they love him because they believe in him. Faith in love, in other words, both in human relationships and in relationships with God as represented by Jesus, are acts of total human commitment that are inseparable from one another. We may speak of the virtues of faith and the virtues of charity as being different, but in fact, in the real world, they are identical. One can no more separate faith and love in God than one can separate faith and love in human relationships.

Many of us grew up believing that faith was agreement with a long list of propositions, much like a true-false test in high school or college. If we could say "true" to everything on the list of things a Catholic had to believe, we had faith; and if we were forced to put "false" or "I don't know" after any of the propositions, then we didn't have faith, and it probably would be a good thing to leave the church. This is not the way, however, that the Bible understands faith. Faith is a commitment to Jesus, to the person of Jesus, made under the force of love—precisely the sort of commitment we read about in the gospel. It is a commitment which may indeed have been preceded by and involve some kind of agreement with propositional assertions. But it goes far beyond that.

We believe in Jesus, we are committed to the Father in heaven, cast in our lot with the Catholic tradition and heritage because, like everybody in love, we realize that there is nothing else to do but to make the commitment. Just as human love, after it has gone a certain distance, compels our commitment even if we still stew and fret about uncertainties and problems, so also does our Christian commitment. It is something that we ultimately feel compelled to make simply because of the attractiveness of God and Jesus and of much of what is the church. Our personality embraces the faith even if our mind is still baffled, intrigued, puzzled, hesitant. The act of faith, then, like all commitments to a loved one, is a leap in the dark. But it is a joyous leap, because it is a leap in the direction of Something and Someone we want. God, Jesus and church have become the indispensable other, and we want that other, regardless of the consequences. The leap of religious faith, then, is almost precisely parallel to the leap of love.

In another passage in the Bible, Jesus asks his apostles if they will join with the others that are walking away from him. Simon Peter, loud and outspoken as always, says, "Lord, to whom shall we go? You have the words of life." So it is with all love. If we give up the one we love, to whom else can we go? Many of those younger Catholics who drifted away from the church in their 20s and early 30s and are now returning are in effect doing the same thing, and making the same choice that is described in the gospel. They return because they discovered how much they did not appreciate what was not only attractive but virtually indispensable. They return not so much to an institution but to a childhood love they had not fully appreciated. They may still have many intellectual problems, difficulties about the Catholic heritage that they still have to work out, but they have decided that the only place to work them out is by being part of the Catholic tradition, by being members in the Catholic community. They understand that the problems of a love relationship are worked out inside the relationship and not by terminating it.

31

The Joy of Love

Hilaire Belloc, the English Catholic writer, in one of his "Cautionary Verses," announces: "Wherever the Catholic sun does shine/ there is music and laughter and good red wine/ At least I've found it so./ Benedicamus Domino." Belloc was unquestionably comparing the festivity of his beloved Catholic Mediterranean culture with the moroseness of some northern European puritanical versions of Protestantism. By those standards, heaven knows, we Catholics are indeed a festive crowd. Yet we are hardly immune from the curse of sour-faced saints. Many of our non-Catholic and non-Christian neighbors and friends would scarcely describe us as easy-going, celebratory, joyous humans. On the contrary, we are often grim, somber and dour, preoccupied with sin, damnation and guilt, solemnly insisting on obedience to the letter of multitudinous rules and laws and so uptight about our faith as to be unable to relax or enjoy ourselves. Those who are attracted to Catholic Christianity and eventually become Catholics rarely mention that the principal appeal is the joyfulness of the Catholics they know. Music, laughter, good red wine? Not so's you'd notice it, unfortunately.

Note the kind of instructions Jesus gives the first ones who are going forth to be associates and colleagues. It would be a mistake to read that gospel passage as merely advice about logistical or financial arrangements. The point is not that the followers of Jesus traveled light; and the lesson for us is not necessarily a vow of poverty. The point is that Jesus' followers were carefree, and the lesson for us is one of joy.

If Christianity has not spread to the ultimate corners of the earth, if many people find its Catholic version to be singularly unattractive, the fault does not reside either in the gospel or in the Catholic Christian heritage, but in Catholic Christians who have not been joyous enough, nor hopeful enough, nor merry enough, nor carefree enough. There is much talk about "evangelization" in the church today, and that is all to the good. The church is in the evangelization business. But sometimes people seem to confuse evangelization with high pressure, mass media publicity or with organizational membership drives, or with "convert-making" techniques. There may not be anything wrong with methods, drives, techniques, and gimmicks (though on occasion there may be), but it is important that every Catholic Christian understand that the essence of evangelization is not a technique, a gimmick, a drive, or a plan; the essence of evangelization is joyous, carefree, happy love. An evangelization campaign which is not animated by such carefree love and not staffed by joyous, happy Christians will simply not work. Indeed, it may very well do more harm than good.

The love must not be forced, must not be phony, must not be the smothering, sticky, sweet love of some religious enthusiasts who oppress other people by their love or by what they pretend is love when it is in fact merely skillful manipulation. It must be *real* love, the kind of love that leaves other human beings free to make their own choices, just as it was quite clear to Jesus' followers that they were to constrain or to compel no one to embrace the gospel. It was a free option to be lovingly offered and lovingly accepted without any constraint, even the constraint that may masquerade as loving affection. We cannot approach other human beings with the pretense of knowing the answers to what life really means if we do not, by the kind of lives we live, demonstrate that our faith does put meaning in our life and makes us more generously loving, more humane, more compassionate and free within our own self-possession and our relationship to others. We cannot short-circuit the process, we cannot substitute high-pressure, sophisticated gimmickry and the hard sell for the witness of a free, mature, generous, loving life.

It might be argued that we Catholic Christians

have a long way to go before we even begin to approach the ideal of joy expressed in "laughter and music and good red wine." Nor would very many people view us as carefree followers of Jesus of the sort described in the gospel. We cannot delay the preaching of the gospel until we become saints ourselves, of course; it would never happen. But we should at least be clear in our own minds as to the kind of lives we ought to live so that our preaching of the gospel will be something more than a mindless bleating of words in an empty hall.

How does one become carefree? Perhaps more to the point, why should one be carefree? Are there not enough cares and worries in the world to keep us mired indefinitely? Is it not false to be joyous? Should we not be somber and serious because that is precisely the appropriate response to the mess the world is in? Is not the sour-faced saint in fact the good Christian? Is not his or her sour face reflecting the disastrous state of the human condition and God's legitimate anger over all the sin in the world? What is there to be all that hopeful about? That question, of course, brings us to the essence of Christianity, a religion whose center is good news. Indeed, the good news is that God's forgiving, reconciling, saving love is far stronger than all the evil, all the tragedy, all the suffering in the world. Even death ultimately yields to the power of God's love. It is just that simple. We believe it, then necessarily we live lives of joy and hopefulness. We will then be truly fundamentally carefree, no matter how many cares there might be in our lives.

32

Martha Versus Mary

One of the aims of the Marriage Encounter movement is promoting conversations between husband and wife. Many people are amazed to discover, in fact, how little they do talk to one another. Many American husbands and wives can live together, produce and raise children, share a common life for many years, indeed be quite fond of each other, and still rarely find the time and the peace and the opportunity to talk about anything more than an immediate problem or the immediate issues of their life. In our society, both men and women, it would seem, are "Marthas," with neither the time, the patience, the opportunity or the skills to develop the "Mary" aspect of their personalities or the Mary aspect of their relationships.

One of the difficulties that we often experience in understanding and appreciating the gospel story of Mary and Martha is that we tend to think of them as different personality types instead of different dimensions of all our personalities. Doubtless there are some people in whom the Martha proclivity is well-developed, if not overdeveloped; and maybe there are a few people (perhaps not all that many in contemporary America) who have become so contemplative that they never get anything done. In fact there is a bit of Martha and a bit of Mary in each of us. If the gospel has any meaning at all for contemporary Americans, it is clearly that we have neglected the Mary aspect of our personality, the Mary aspect of our life, and the Mary aspect of our relationships, particularly our closest and most intimate relationships.

The Martha in us is busy about many things— keeping the house in some kind of order, doing the job, earning the money, paying the bills, promoting a career, chauffering the children, going to meetings, getting ready for school, cutting the lawn, planning the party, getting in the golf game, making a tennis date, keeping all the obligations and the responsibilities. Life may be more affluent now than it used to be, but it is also more complicated. We may have to work at our jobs less than those who once put in a twelve-hour day, but our so-called "free" time is not that free. It is hurry, rush, wait for the weekend, and then find that it slips through our fingers and it's Monday morning again, back to the same old routine.

We live lives, as James Thurber said of "noisy desperation." It is the Martha in us who responds to that noisy desperation with increased tension, more anxiety, and, quite possibly, more noise as the desperation level mounts. It is easy to make fun of the Martha lurking inside each of

us, because lives of noisy desperation are funny
in a gruesome sort of way. Still, somebody has to
cut the lawn, somebody has to plan the party,
somebody has to get things ready for school,
somebody has to earn the money, cook the
meals, pay the bills. Indeed, if we take the gospel
about the good Samaritan seriously, somebody
has to see that the healing gets done, and healing
requires time, energy, and effort. Mary doesn't
heal, Martha does. If we emphasize the impor-
tance of the Mary dimension, the reason is that
in our particular society there are few people
who err by excess when it comes to the Mary aspect of their lives. There are few people who are
too quiet, too contemplative, too reflective, too
much addicted to silence and loving contemplation.

For us Americans, activity is easy and contemplation is difficult. We always mean to find time
to think, to read, to relax, to have quiet and
serious conversation with those we love, to do
some reflective prayer perhaps. But there are so
many other things going on that when life does
quiet down at the end of the day, we are so exhausted that our temptation is to flip on the television set to dull the pain of exhaustion. To simply sit and contemplate love is indeed attractive;
we would be delighted to do it, if only there were
more time. Maybe when the kids are in school,
or raised, or during our next vacation, then we'll

be able to do it. Not now, we don't have the time.

There is a tremendous resurgence of interest in prayer in the United States today. Much of that resurgence, it is to be feared, is Martha-like prayer—noisy, vocal, striving prayer. Prayers of quiet, of solitude, prayers of reflection are rare. Most of us are not very good at doing that kind of prayer. The link between reflective prayer, quiet contemplation, and communication between husbands and wives is not as intricate or complicated as it might appear. One has to acquire certain habits of reflection, a certain sense of peace, a certain ability to pull back from the immediate Martha demands in order to establish communication between the Mary in us and the Mary in our spouse. It isn't easy to do, and it probably cannot be done unless husband and wife try to do it together. They both have to learn how to be quiet together before they are able to talk together; they both have to learn the patience and discipline of silence before they can enjoy the pleasure of reflection. There is no way that skill can be acquired except through practice and work. A few moments of silent prayer each day, some of it alone and some of it together, is absolutely indispensable for a man and woman who wish to improve the quality of their conversation and the quality of their silence, as well as the quality of their life together.

We will continue to be Marthas, allowing the

Martha within us to dominate, unless we are able to mobilize resources to support and liberate the Mary within us. Those who are not married need the support of their friends, those who are married need above all the support of their spouse. The question is whether we are willing to seek and whether we are willing to give the necessary help so that the quiet, sensitive, peaceful, loving Mary that is in each of us might be freed.

33

Careless With God

There is a certain kind of person who is always scheming, plotting, crafting. This person may be a business entrepreneur, an inventor, a story-teller, or a salesperson, but he/she is so preoccu-pied, almost obsessed, by his/her craft that he/she cannot leave it behind when the day's work is done. He/she takes it to dinners and par-ties, ponders it while driving, thinks about it even in the shower, and dreams about it at night. The legend is told about Thomas Aquinas that once he was invited to dinner at the home of the King of France. He fell silent halfway through the meal. The other guests continued eating while the massive Dominican stared blankly off into space. Suddenly he pounded the table and announced to the other guests, "That's the an-swer to the Manichaeans!" The King, himself a saint, was a forgiving host. He promptly called one of his scribes so that the distinguished Ital-ian philosopher might record the answer while it was still fresh.

The comparison between shrewd human be-havior on secular matters and sloppy, lacka-daisical indifferences on religious matters pre-occupied Jesus. Several times during the course of his ministry he returned to the subject, marveling at how industrious and shrewd we are about the things of this world and how casual and lackadaisical we are about our relationship with God. Jesus is not criticizing salespersons, craftsmen, philosophers, or candidates for their "craftiness." On the contrary, he is holding up their diligence and cleverness for our imitation in matters of the spirit. He is shaking his head in dismay that we don't imitate them. A story-teller with an idea for a novel will get up in the middle of the night, stumble through the darkness for a pen and notebook to jot down a bit of dialogue while he/she still has it in mind. A businessman will run the risk of being late for supper (and all the attendant trouble this may cause him!) to return a call from an important client he has been trying to reach all day. Which one of us will invest that kind of energy and that kind of sacrifice into squeezing out five minutes each day for prayer and reflection that may be necessary to sustain our relationship to God?

A man who is courting a woman leaves no stone unturned to impress her with his kindness, sensitivity, consideration, affection. A woman who is courting a man thinks no preparation too demanding in order that she might appear bright, fresh, charming, witty. Later in life, when the same man and woman are going through the painful joys of reconciliation, they again lean over backwards to be careful, considerate, and tender. For whatever may have gone wrong, this is still the important relationship in their lives, and they are willing to spend enormous amounts of time, energy, and effort to keep it alive.

Who acts this way with God? Of course, we don't see him; we are not usually conscious of his physical presence in our home. He doesn't send us large checks periodically. He has, of course, created the splendid world in which we live, given us our life, provided us with the food we eat, the air we breathe, the water we drink, and the friends who love us. He has left around all kinds of signs and hints of his affection and concern, but somehow these don't make quite the impact on us that he seems to hope for. We are not indifferent to God; we squeeze him in when there's time, but we haven't yet been able to give him top priority. Maybe next week, next month, next year we'll have more time for God and calculate shrewdly, cleverly, industriously how to respond to his loving goodness. But there's still time. Why hurry?

What we miss when we become casual and careless with God is not merely or, in one sense, not even mainly happiness in the life that is to come. We all know from experience that when we do squeeze in some time each day for prayerful reflection, for communication and even communion with God, life is a lot more peaceful, more rewarding, more tranquil. Prayer does not help us to live. We don't pray because it will make us live better; we pray because we respond to love. But having responded to love, our lives become happier and more peaceful. We all know that, and yet we do not, to use that awful word, "prioritize" our prayer so that it is protected from the distractions that can destroy it.

34
Families Fight

The family that doesn't fight must be viewed with suspicion, because beneath the apparently peaceful and serene outside, there is enormous anger bubbling up. Under their sweetly calm exteriors, the members of a non-fighting family may have murder on their minds. Stay away from the families in which husband and wife, parents and children, grandparents and parents never seem to have any conflict at all. You might get in the way when a modern-day Lizzie Borden begins to swing her deadly ax.

One of the major contributions that modern psychology has made to our understanding of family life is that it has helped us to realize that conflict among people in intimate relationships is as natural as breathing. Sometimes the friction is coped with easily. Awakened from his sleep, Joseph uncomplainedly took the child and the child's mother and went into Egypt. Joseph and Mary protested, if not with anger, then with an obvious sense of hurt when Jesus deserted them to remain in the temple. The holy family did not shout and rant and smash dishes, but there was tension and friction, because each of the members had different perspectives and different obligations.

We ought not "pretty up" our picture of the life of the holy family so that they become super-human, quite unlike us and of no relevance to our lives. There may not have been violent out-bursts of temper, but there were misunderstand-ings, confusion, and friction for which we have evidence in the scriptures. Hence we can con-clude that family tensions and family conflicts are not necessarily sinful. While the loss of con-trol may be wrong, the working out of family tensions is not wrong, and the solution to family fights is not to repress the different perspectives, the different goals, the different emotions under a phony cover of sweetness and light. Rather, the response to inevitable family conflict is to develop the skills of loving reconciliation which are essential if our family relationships are to continue to be what modern research has dem-onstrated them to be—the most important chan-nels of grace in the lives of most human beings.

In their book, *Marital Intimacy: A Catholic Per-spective* (Drs. Joan Anzia and Mary Durkin), using both social science and theology, describe four phases in the cycle of family intimacy, a cycle that applies especially to the relationship between husband and wife but also to the rela-tionship between parents and children—even when the children have themselves become adults. The four phases are: "falling in love," "settling down," "bottoming out," and "begin-

ning again." The authors argue that a propensity
to such a cycle relationship seems built into the
human personality. Our romances, our love affairs are inevitably stormy, with ups and downs,
high tides, ebb tides, moments of joy and moments of near despair. Sometimes the cycle is
short, sometimes quite long. There are large
cycles that go on for many years and mini-cycles
within the larger ones that represent the daily,
weekly, or monthly ups and downs in the husband-wife, parent-child relationship.

All of us who have families or are part of families are aware that we have our moments of falling in love, of settling into a routine, of hitting a
rock bottom of conflict or even hatred, and then,
perhaps, beginning again. The love of the holy
family is offered for our consideration not because our love can be expected to be as intense
or as effective as their love, but rather because
they reveal to us God's love and the possibility,
in God's love, of forgiving and being forgiven.
The holy family is not so much an example to be
imitated, even though we are aware that that
family had some tensions and frictions, but a
sacrament, a hint of the secret of God's love because Jesus and Mary and Joseph loved each
other the way they did only because God loved
them and because they trusted completely and
totally in that love.

The promise of the holy family is not that the

cycles of ups and downs can be eliminated from our own family life. Rather, it is the promise that God's love is so powerful that we can overcome the terrifying conflict which threatens to destroy our lives and we can begin again. We can forgive and be forgiven just as God has forgiven us, and we are free in the love of Christmastime to fall in love again. The holy family is not God's guarantee that family fights can be or will be eliminated; rather, the holy family is God's guarantee that love can be born anew. No matter how harsh, how bitter, how hateful, how destructive the conflict is, we can still fall in love again.

35

The Problem of Intimate Enemies

Most of us can remember the shifting alliances of early childhood. Little kids, for reasons that may seem wholly irrational to their parents and are not altogether clear to the kids themselves, decide that they like some of their peers and don't like others. The ones they don't like might just as well not exist except for those times when they throw taunts or snowballs across the schoolyard. Then a metamorphosis comes, the alliances change, and enemies become friends, friends become enemies. Kids who were no good at all suddenly acquire great virtue and attractiveness, while those who were inseparable companions become targets for the whirling snowballs. Kids are not bothered by the inconsistency of logic in the conversion of enemies to friends, because being an enemy doesn't mean as much to them as it does to adults. Hence they are able to find attractiveness in those whom they had not previously liked with far greater ease than we do.

Enemies can be very useful either as scapegoats or as reality checks. It is fundamentally unhealthy to blame our problems on our enemies. Doubtless there are some things that happen to us in life that are done by real live enemies, people who do not like us and who are out to get us. But most of our problems are not caused by others as much as by ourselves. We are our own worst enemies in the sense that we generally manage to do more harmful things to ourselves than to our worst enemies. Indeed, with a friend like most of us are to ourselves we don't need enemies.

Scapegoating enemies is usually just plain nonsense. Much more healthy is to think of the enemy as a reality check, as someone who reveals to us both our strengths and our weaknesses, strengths which they envy and weaknesses which they see much more clearly than we do. An enemy's view of us is like a distorting mirror in an amusement park; it exaggerates, twists, accentuates, caricatures. Yet an enemy may often see us more clearly than we see ourselves. We should listen to our enemies so that we might better see ourselves.

The gospel command that we should love our enemies is, for most of us, not all that difficult, because we have few, if any, enemies—at least not very intense ones. Our lives are not of sufficient magnitude to stir up much more than a little envy. Terrible, implacable, hate-filled enemies are few and far between. The real enemy for most of us is the intimate other, the person or persons who are close to us and in whom we excite strong feelings of ambivalence—affection and repugnance, respect and fear, love and hatred. The enemy that we are to love, if we follow the gospel, is most often the intimate enemy—the parent, the spouse, the child—who loves us but who can't stand us, who adores us but is infuriated by us, who would give his or her life for us but finds life with us difficult, who knows more about us that is good than does anyone else in the world but also more about us that is bad. Similarly, we, in our relationship to the intimate enemies we both love and hate, know they mean everything to us but we can't stand them.

Ambivalence is not wrong; it is an inevitable aspect of the human condition. Any two persons thrust together in an intimate relationship are bound to get on each other's nerves. Indeed, the first step in dealing with ambivalence frequently is to be able to acknowledge its existence. Nor should we ever expect to eliminate it completely from our human intimacy. The trick with ambivalence is to keep it under control and to learn from it, to be able to talk about it, profit from it, grow through it. Being able to love the intimate enemy as we love ourselves involves understanding that the other is a self too, caught in the same ambivalences in which we are caught, seeking to transcend those ambivalences so that he or she can love us the same way he or she loves the self.

The mandate to love our enemies and to do good to those who harm us is not often thought of as applying to closest human intimacies, those between, let us say, parents and children, between husband and wife. Yet, indeed, the wisdom of returning good for evil makes more sense in these relationships than in any others; for if the other does evil to us and we return that evil with good, then the other will love us all the more and the relationship will grow and flourish. We must examine our consciences and ask ourselves how often in our relationships with the intimate other do we return evil for evil, and how often do we return good for evil?

36

Love Binds and Drives Apart

The movie *Altered States* tells the story of a scientist who by the use of a special drug and an
isolation tank contrives to return to the primal
moment of creation, the beginning of everything. He regresses to a protohominid, apelike
condition; and then he goes back to the original
amoeba from which life sprang; then still further
back to the verge of the darkness that existed before creation. It is all very spectacular with chill-
ing special effects and a scary conclusion that
shows him the darkness beyond the primal in-
stant during which everything began. He is
saved from a descent into nothingness by the
love of his wife who reaches out her hand and
pulls him back. The metaphysics and the theology of *Altered States* is slippery. Clearly before
there was anything there was nothing, and nothing is terrifying. But to say that before creation
there was nothing does not mean life is without
purpose or meaning or that there was no Being.
However, the human psychology of the film was
absolutely correct. The half-mad scientist is
pulled back into his present existence to find
purpose and meaning in that existence by an act
of generous and self-sacrificing love. Love is the

binding power of the universe; it holds everything together—not only human beings but also
the very cosmos itself. The tiniest subatomic
particle to the largest cluster of galaxies is
finally bound and preserved from dissolution,
kept in existence by the first act of love, love that
binds together the community that we call God:
Father, Son and Holy Spirit.

Love is a primal energy that both binds together and drives apart. One might think of
gravity which attracts all the objects in the universe to one another as a form of love. One
might also think of the centrifugal force, the "big
bang" that sends all the galaxies of the universe
spinning out from one another forever farther
into nothingness as also a manifestation of love.
For love both drives apart and pulls together; it
does not necessarily drive us apart in destructive ways. In the Trinity, for example, the love
that binds together the three persons does not
disintegrate the distinctivenss of each. Quite the
contrary, the binding love of the three persons
makes each of them more powerfully unique,
more intimately related to one another, and yet
more distinctively and powerfully themselves.
So it is with human love at its finest. It integrates
and binds together in powerful, unbreakable
chains human personalities that are attracted to
one another. However, the power of human

love, if it is truly liberating and unselfish human love, forces the partners back upon their own selves both because one must be strongly and uniquely oneself to respond to the demands of the loved one and because in the confidence and the validation that comes from the other's esteem we have the courage to be uniquely and especially ourselves. In human love, as well as in the love of the church, we are drawn powerfully to one another and yet forced back firmly and decisively on the uniqueness of our own selfhood.

The love of the Trinity, then, is revealed to us not to overwhelm us with its mystery or to blind us with its splendor, much less to impose upon us a test of faith. It is rather to tell us something about the meaning of love. True love binds powerfully, but it does not create dependence; rather true love demands, challenges, and reinforces independence. True love does not take away the freedom we have or demand that we abdicate it; rather it makes us more radically free than ever before, more confident in ourselves than ever before.

All human love is a mixture of freedom and restriction, of independence and dependence, of attraction which liberates and attraction which needs to dominate. The passionate, loving energy of the Trinity is less a model to be imitated than a guarantee of liberating, generous, enhancing love as a possibility in our universe.

In the most important loves of our life, how much honesty is there? How much freedom? How much of the powerful attraction that both binds us together and compels us to be distinctly and uniquely ourselves?

37

Love in the Eucharist

A husband and wife are in the midst of a quarrel, one that has been building up for weeks, perhaps even for months or years. They are, however, scheduled to go out to dinner with another couple. The customs of our society being what they are, it is necessary to pretend that no conflict exists. So the man and woman go through the motions of a relaxed, pleasant, fun-filled evening, even though they are inwardly boiling at one another and frustrated by the need to pretend. They are acting out, in other words, a ritual of love when the love between them is dormant at least.

Such situations—and they happen in all marriages and in many friendships—demonstrate that sharing a meal is an act of intimacy. We incorporate food into our body together with somebody else while at the same time we are, as it were, incorporating that other person into our personality as a friend, companion, partner, one who is intimate to us in our life. There are varying degrees of intimacy, depending upon the partner and the meal. The sharing of the food, however, and the sharing of the personality are closely linked phenomena. Just as we want to share food with those with whom we are inti-

mate, so we tend to be intimate with those with
whom we share food. Such things are not absolutely necessary, of course, but they represent
strong propensities and inclinations of our personality. They are the ordinary, the commonplace way of doing things.

So it was not accidental that Jesus directed
that the Eucharist be the memory of his presence among us and that he represents himself to
us in the Eucharist. The Eucharist is a banquet,
it is a ritual which re-enacts, reaffirms, and re-
validates our incorporation into the body of
those who are the friends of Jesus, that group
who by consuming the Word of God and by consuming the Eucharist are united in loving intimacy with Jesus, with one another, and with the
Father in heaven.

The love we celebrate and reinforce in the
Eucharist, however, is not easy. No love is ever
easy, because the attractive, repellant powers involved in love are so powerful. We are drawn to
one another and we are afraid of one another.
We want to give ourselves, but we fear being
hurt, we want to be united with the other, yet
the other terrifies us. We want the ecstasy that
comes from union, but we do not want to pay
the price of surrender. We want to run toward
the other, but when we get close we want to flee.
We want to incorporate the other and be incor-

porated by the other; we are terrified, though, that we will lose our identity by such an act. So we compromise, not giving ourselves over to complete love but also not retreating into hate—a mixture of love and hate, with love being just a little bit stronger keeping the intimacy from breaking apart. It characterizes our marital loves, our close friendships, relationships between parents and children, and relationships with our fellow Christians and with God.

We eat our common meals together, whether they be at church or at home, harboring our petty resentments and our intense affections, but trying to keep everything low key, casual, relaxed; we try to "cool it" with one another and with God because that way we're safe. It protects us from the roller coaster of up-and-down emotion which is inevitable when we permit love the freedom to flourish. We don't unincorporate ourselves, but we don't incorporate ourselves either; we don't withdraw from our communities, but we don't commit ourselves intensely to them. Being afraid of both heaven and hell, in other words, we search for limbo. We eat the bread of eternal life but cool our consumption down to an empty Sunday Morning or Saturday evening ritual. There are no implications for the rest of our lives. Not wanting to be hot or cold, we are lukewarm, and we try to forget that

Jesus said he would vomit the lukewarm out of his mouth.

To love someone else is a risk. The only true lover is a gambler, sometimes a reckless one. It matters not whether we love God or another human being. To act out the ritual which we celebrate in the Eucharist or at an intimate meal is to put ourselves on the line, to risk everything on a single throw of the dice, to "go for broke" with our personality. The potential payoff is great, but so are the potential losses. If there is no touch of the reckless gambler, the "go-for-broke" risk-taker in our personalities, we will never give ourselves in love and never trust the gift of love from someone else. Then we will settle for the every-day routine of going to work, cleaning the house, cooking the meal, putting the children to bed, watching television, going to mass on Saturday or Sunday, convinced that this is what life is really all about, closing our ears to the promises of the gospel and to the challenge implied in every Eucharistic banquet, the challenge of risk-taking and gambling, and the reckless search for love. Such is a safe life, but it is a life in which the yearnings of the human heart, the anguish of the human soul, the desperate hunger of the human personality are stifled because they suggest danger and possible defeat.

If we really believed the Eucharist was the bread of eternal life and that when we ate it we were guaranteed through our union with God and Jesus that we would be raised up on the last day, then we would not be afraid to risk ourselves in human love. Our human loves are weak, mediocre, compromising, superficial, routine things when we don't trust the divine love which has been offered to us.